Careers in Focus

ANIMATION

Ferguson
An imprint of Infobase Publishing

Careers in Focus: Animation

Copyright © 2010 by Infobase Publishing

All rights reserved. No part of this book may be reproduced or utilized in any form or by any means, electronic or mechanical, including photocopying, recording, or by any information storage or retrieval systems, without permission in writing from the publisher. For information contact:

Ferguson
An imprint of Infobase Publishing
132 West 31st Street
New York NY 10001

Library of Congress Cataloging-in-Publication Data

Careers in focus. Animation. — 1st ed.
   p. cm.
  Includes index.
  ISBN-13: 978-0-8160-8015-1 (hardcover : alk. paper)
  ISBN-10: 0-8160-8015-1 (hardcover : alk. paper) 1. Animated films—Vocational guidance—Juvenile literature. 2. Animation (Cinematography—Vocational guidance—Juvenile literature. 3. Motion picture industry—Vocational guidance—Juvenile literature. I. Title: Animation.
  NC1765.C37 2010
  791.43'34023—dc22   2009049377

Ferguson books are available at special discounts when purchased in bulk quantities for businesses, associations, institutions, or sales promotions. Please call our Special Sales Department in New York at (212) 967-8800 or (800) 322-8755.

You can find Ferguson on the World Wide Web at http://www.fergpubco.com

Text design by David Strelecky
Composition by Mary Susan Ryan-Flynn
Cover printed by Art Print, Taylor, PA
Book printed and bound by Maple Press, York, PA
Date printed: November 2010
Printed in the United States of America

10 9 8 7 6 5 4 3 2

This book is printed on acid-free paper.

All links and Web addresses were checked and verified to be correct at the time of publication. Because of the dynamic nature of the Web, some addresses and links may have changed since publication and may no longer be valid.

Table of Contents

Introduction

Animation of some type or another can be found almost every-where you look these days—from computer and video games and animated commercials, to television shows such as *The Simpsons* and, of course, feature films, such as *Shrek* and *WALL-E*. Animation is also used in music videos, on Web sites, and in medical, education, architectural, and military training simulations, among other uses. *Careers in Focus: Animation* describes a variety of careers in animation-related industries.

According to AnimationMentor.com, the top employment sectors for animation professionals are: 1) computer and video games; 2) feature films; 3) advertising/commercials; and 4) television shows. Employment opportunities for animation professionals are available at game companies, animation studios, software developers, advertising agencies, colleges and universities, law firms, marketing research firms, publishing companies, and many other employers.

While a majority of careers in animation require artistic and/or technological talent, there are also opportunities for people with backgrounds in business, marketing, customer service, and other fields. Earnings for animation professionals range from $25,000 for new video game testers to $200,000 or more for intellectual property lawyers and top designers, business managers, marketing research analysts, software engineers, graphics programmers, and directors.

A few of these careers—such as modelers, supporting artists, and sound workers—require some postsecondary training or an associate's degree. Many positions in this industry (such as programmer, editor, writer, and computer and video game designer) require a minimum of a bachelor's degree. Others, such as animators and scriptwriters, do not require a college education although many of the top professionals in these fields combine a college education with exceptional creative talent. The career of intellectual property lawyer requires a law degree. Animation professors at top schools typically have a master's degree or a doctorate.

According to the Entertainment Software Association, the U.S. computer and video game industry had software sales of $9.5 billion in 2007—an increase of more than 300 percent since 1996. Employment in this industry is expected to continue to be strong over the next decade.

Advances in computer technology have also helped create a revolution in other animation-related industries. Animation is increasingly used in commercials and training simulations used by a variety of industries. These technological innovations have also prompted strong growth in the animated film and television industries and have created several noteworthy trends. First, viewing options for animated films and shows have expanded. In addition to viewing in theaters and on television, animated features and shorts are now available for delivery by mail; for download onto computers, MP3 players, and mobile devices; and for streaming on the Internet—which has increased the number of animated films and shorts that are being produced. Second, animation audiences have changed. Animation is not just for children anymore; high-quality animation in a variety of genres is now available for adults. Two examples of animated features for adults include *Persepolis* and *Waltz With Bashir*, which were nominated for Academy Awards in 2007 and 2008, respectively. *Family Guy* and *King of the Hill* are two examples of animated television shows that have been created for adult audiences. Finally, an increasing number of animated movies are being created in digital 3D. In 2009 DreamWorks Animation SKG, one of the leading animation studios in the world, began creating all of its animated films in 3D. As a result of these trends, opportunities should be strong in animation-related industries through 2016.

Some of the articles in *Careers in Focus: Animation* appear in Ferguson's *Encyclopedia of Careers and Vocational Guidance*, but have been updated and revised with the latest information from the U.S. Department of Labor, professional organizations, and other sources. Others have been created especially for this book.

The following paragraphs detail the sections and features that appear in the book.

The **Quick Facts** section provides a brief summary of the career, including recommended school subjects, personal skills, work environment, minimum educational requirements, salary ranges, certification or licensing requirements, and employment outlook. This section also provides acronyms and identification numbers for the following government classification indexes: the Dictionary of Occupational Titles (DOT), the Guide for Occupational Exploration (GOE), the National Occupational Classification (NOC) Index, and the Occupational Information Network (O*NET)-Standard Occupational Classification System (SOC) index. The DOT, GOE, and O*NET-SOC indexes have been created by the U.S. government; the NOC index is Canada's career classification system. Readers can use the identification numbers listed in the Quick Facts section to access further information about a career. Print editions of the DOT (*Dictionary of Occupational Titles*. Indianapolis, Ind.: JIST Works, 1991) and GOE (*Guide for Occupational Exploration*. Indianapolis, Ind.: JIST Works, 2001) are available at libraries. Electronic versions of the NOC (http://www23.hrdc-drhc.gc.ca) and O*NET-SOC (http://online.onetcenter.org) are available on the Internet. When no DOT, GOE, NOC, or O*NET-SOC numbers are present, this means that the U.S. Department of Labor or Human Resources Development Canada have not created a numerical designation for this career. In this instance, you will see the acronym "N/A," or not available.

The **Overview** section is a brief introductory description of the duties and responsibilities involved in this career. Oftentimes, a career may have a variety of job titles. When this is the case, alternative career titles are presented. The **History** section describes the history of the particular job as it relates to the overall development of its industry or field. **The Job** describes the primary and secondary duties of the job. **Requirements** discusses high school and postsecondary education and training requirements, any certification or licensing that is necessary, and other personal requirements for success in the job. **Exploring** offers suggestions on how to gain experience in or knowledge of the particular job before making a firm educational and financial commitment. The focus is on what can be done while still in high school (or in the early years of college) to gain a better understanding of the job. The **Employers** section gives an overview of typical places of employment for the job. **Starting Out** discusses the best ways to land that first job, be it through the college career services office, newspaper ads, Internet employment sites, or personal contact. The **Advancement** section describes what kind of career path to expect from the job and how to get there. **Earnings** lists salary ranges and describes the typical fringe benefits. The **Work Environment** section describes the typical surroundings and conditions of employment—whether indoors or outdoors, noisy or quiet, social or independent. Also discussed are typical hours worked, any seasonal fluctuations, and the stresses and strains of the job. The **Outlook** section summarizes the job in terms of the general economy and industry projections. For the most part, Outlook information is obtained from the U.S. Bureau of Labor Statistics and is supplemented by information gathered from professional associations. Job growth terms follow those used in the *Occupational Outlook Handbook*. Growth described as "much faster than the average" means an increase of 21 percent or more. Growth described as "faster than the average" means an increase of 14 to 20 percent. Growth described as "about as fast as the average" means an increase of 7 to 13 percent. Growth described as "more slowly than the average" means an increase of 3 to 6 percent. "Little or no change" means a decrease of 2 percent to an increase of 2 percent. "Decline" means a decrease of 3 percent or more. Each article ends with **For More Information,** which lists organizations that provide information on training, education, internships, scholarships, and job placement.

Careers in Focus: Animation also includes photographs, informative sidebars, and interviews with professionals in the field.

Animators

OVERVIEW

Animators are artists who design the cartoons that appear in movies, television shows, commercials, music videos, training applications for scientific fields and the military, and in other settings. Approximately 87,000 animators and multimedia artists are employed in the United States. Slightly more than 9,000 are employed in the film and television industries.

HISTORY

Frenchman Èmile Reynaud created what is considered the first animated cartoon in 1892. He created the cartoon by drawing and hand-painting images on film paper and using a praxinoscope, an optical instrument he invented to create the illusion of movement, or animation. *Fantasmagorie,* considered the first fully animated film, was made by French director Èmile Courtet (aka Èmile Cohl) in 1908.

As Hollywood grew in the early 1900s, so did companies that created cartoons, although these animated films were silent (just like all movies of the time). Bray Studios in New York City was one of the best-known cartoon studios of the time. It operated from circa 1915 to the late 1920s. Some of its cartoons include *Out of the Inkwell* (1916), *Electric Bell* (1918), and *If You Could Shrink* (1920).

Walt Disney also got his start in the business around this time. In 1923 he sold his first cartoon, *Alice's Wonderland,* to a distributor and soon after founded Disney Brothers Cartoon Studio (later renamed Walt Disney Studios) with his brother, Roy. By the late 1920s "talkies" had replaced silent films and Walt Disney had cre-

Animation Glossary

2D animation The creation of moving pictures in two dimensions, which can be accomplished using computers or through the traditional method of hand-drawing hundreds or even thousands of individual images, or "frames." These frames are then transferred onto clear plastic sheets called *cels*, colored by hand, and filmed in sequence over a painted background image. Showing these frames at a rate of 24 or more per second results in the viewer seeing what appears to be continuous motion.

3D animation The creation of moving pictures in three dimensions, with the additional dimension of depth that is lacking in 2D productions. Early 3D animation essentially consisted of stop-motion animation of 3D models, but the advent of computers has made it easier and faster to achieve even more realistic 3D effects.

background A drawing, usually in watercolor, acrylic, or oil, which is the part of a given segment in an animated film that is the farthest to the rear. A series of celluloid sheets, or "cels," is photographed over the background to create a scene or scenes in the film.

cel A piece of clear plastic, also known as celluloid, containing the images that are placed over a background to be photographed in succession to form the action of a completed animated film. The outline of the image is applied to the front of the cel, while the colors are painted on the back (although certain colors, such as black, are sometimes painted onto the front for glare reduction).

CGI Acronym for "computer-generated imagery," which refers to any artwork or animation created with computers. The term *CGI* can apply to both 2D and 3D animation, although it is most commonly used to refer to 3D.

character animation A specialized area of the animation process involving the depiction of thought and emotion by characters in addition to mere movement, a process made famous by the Walt Disney Studios in its productions such as *Three Little Pigs*, *Snow White and the Seven Dwarfs*, *Pinocchio*, and *Dumbo*.

claymation One of the most common forms of stop-motion animation in which the objects being photographed are made of clay; popularized by the *Gumby* animated series.

compositing   The process of incorporating all of the elements of a scene in an animated film together (the animation sequences, the background, and the overlays and underlays in the scene are brought together and positioned correctly, the camera frame is set, and any necessary computer-generated effects are added) before sending them to the next step of "rendering," or creating an image.

computer animation   The creation of moving images through the use of computers. These images can be created in either two or three dimensions and can be applied to Web design, video games, movies, special effects, or cartoons.

demo reel   A collection of prior work by an artist or animator, compiled on VHS, CD, DVD, or another medium; often provided by job seekers to potential employers in the animation industry.

Flash   A multimedia platform (incorporating text, audio, video, animation, and interactivity) distributed by Adobe Systems that has become a popular method of adding animation and interactive features to Web pages; it is also widely used for broadcast animation work.

frame   A single drawing or image that is placed in sequence with other drawings to create the illusion of movement in an animated production.

stop-motion animation   Animation produced by arranging actual objects, taking a picture of them, repositioning the objects with slight differences, then taking another picture of them, and so on, with the end result being a series of consecutive images that create the illusion of motion when viewed in sequence.

storyboard   A visual plan of all the scenes and shots in an animated production, it lays out the story as well as dialogue and instructions regarding framing, action, camera angles, transitions between shots, music, and sound effects.

timeline   A horizontal representation of the elements of a scene in an animated film; a frame-by-frame layout of all animation occurring over a specific period of time in the production. Timelines can be numbered by frame, by second (or other time interval), or both.

ated the cartoon character, Mickey Mouse, which still entertains young and old to this day.

The 1930s and 1940s are considered the golden age of animation. The Walt Disney Studios dominated the industry during these decades. During this time, it created the first animated feature film, *Snow White and the Seven Dwarfs*—which debuted in 1937. The animated film was so groundbreaking that the Academy of Motion Pictures and Sciences gave it a special award in 1938, stating: "to Walt Disney for *Snow White and the Seven Dwarfs,* recognized as a significant screen innovation which has charmed millions and pioneered a great new entertainment field for the motion picture cartoon." Walt Disney Studios went on to create many other animated feature-length classics, including *Pinocchio, Fantasia,* and *Dumbo.*

The popularity of television in the 1950s caused a decline in interest in theatrical cartoons and feature films that lasted into the 1980s. Many consider the release of *Who Framed Roger Rabbit?* by Walt Disney Studios in 1988 as the beginning of a renaissance in animation that continues to this day with highly popular animated features such as *Toy Story, Finding Nemo,* and *WALL-E.* Major animation trends over the last two decades include the popularity of adult-oriented animation, such as *The Simpsons* and *South Park;* the emergence of anime (Japanese-based [although the phenomena has spread throughout Asia], high-quality animation in a variety of genres that is geared not just toward children but also toward adults); the creation of cable networks, such as Nickelodeon and the Cartoon Network, that offer animation as much or all of their programming; and the rise of computer-generated animation, which allows animators infinite creative options and the ability to complete animated features in far less time than by using traditional methods, such as cel animation.

THE JOB

Animators design the cartoons that appear in films and television shows. They also create the digital effects for many commercials, medical simulations, and training tools used in a variety of industries and the military. Making a big-budget animated film, such as *WALL-E, Ratatouille, A Bug's Life,* or *Shrek,* requires a team of many creative people. Each animator on the team works on one small part of the film. On a small production, animators may be involved in many different aspects of the project's development.

An animated film begins with a script. *Scriptwriters,* sometimes known as *screenwriters,* plan the story line, or plot, and write it with dialogue and narration. *Art directors* and *production designers* read the script and decide how the film should look—should it be realistic, futuristic, or humorous? They then draw some of the characters and backgrounds. These designs are then passed on to a *storyboard artist* who illustrates the whole film in a series of frames, similar to a very long comic strip. Based on this storyboard, an artist can then create a detailed layout.

The most common form of animation is cel animation, but this method has changed greatly as a result of the emergence of computers. Animators examine the script, the storyboard, and the layout, and begin to prepare the finished artwork frame-by-frame, or cell-by-cell. Some animators create the "key" drawings—these are the drawings that capture the characters' main expressions and gestures at important parts in the plot. Other animation professionals called *inbetweeners* create the "in between" drawings—the drawings that fill in the spaces between one key drawing and the next. The thousands of final black and white cells are then scanned into a computer. Some animators forego creating on paper altogether and instead use computer software to draw directly into a computer system. In computer or digital animation, the animator creates all the images directly on the computer screen. Computer programs can create effects like shadows, reflections, distortions, and dissolves. Animators are relying increasingly on computers in various

A lead animator at a design company works to animate a Kellogg's cereal character. *(Bill Klotz, AP Photo/Finance and Commerce)*

Did You Know?

Animators rank among the happiest workers in the world, according to a 2008 survey by AnimationMentor.com. Fifty-nine percent of professional animators said that they "enjoyed their work and are proud of the work they do." More than 80 percent planned to continue working in the field. These statistics compare favorably to a national poll of workers conducted by the University of Chicago in 2007. Clergy (67.2 percent) and firefighters (57.2 percent) reported being "very happy" with their jobs.

Source: AnimationMentor.com

areas of production; in fact it is estimated that 95 percent of animation is now created using computers. Computers are used to color animation art, whereas formerly, every frame was painted by hand. Computers also help animators create special effects and even entire films. (One program, Macromedia's Flash, has given rise to an entire Internet cartoon subculture.)

In stop-motion animation, an object, such as a clay creature or doll, is photographed, moved slightly, and photographed again. The process is repeated hundreds of thousands of times. Movies, such as *Chicken Run, The Nightmare Before Christmas, James and the Giant Peach,* and *Coraline,* were animated this way.

REQUIREMENTS

High School

In high school take art, of course, as well as computer classes. Math classes, such as algebra and geometry, will also be helpful. If your school offers animation and graphic design classes, be sure to take those.

Postsecondary Training

You do not need a college degree to become an animator, but most animators today have one. There are a number of animation programs offered at universities and art institutes across the country. You may choose to pursue an associate's, bachelor's, a master's of fine art, or a Ph.D. in computer animation, digital art, graphic design, or art. Some of today's top computer animators are self-taught or have learned their skills on the job—although formal animation education is becoming increasingly popular as competition increases for jobs in the field. Animation World Network offers a database of animation schools at its Web site, http://schools.awn.com. Additionally, aspiring animators should learn as many different software packages as possible, including Maya, PhotoShop, Final Cut, Premiere, and After Effects.

Other Requirements

You must be very creative to be successful as an animator. In addition to having artistic talent, you must be able to generate ideas, although it is not unusual for animators to collaborate with writers for ideas. You must have a good sense of humor (or a good dramatic sense) and an observant eye to detect people's distinguishing characteristics and society's interesting attributes or incongruities.

You also need to be flexible. Because your art is commercial, you must be willing to accommodate your employers' desires if you are to build a broad clientele and earn a decent living. You must be able to take suggestions and rejections gracefully.

You should also have extensive knowledge of animation software and be willing to continue to learn throughout your career since animation and computer technology changes almost constantly.

EXPLORING

Ask your high school art or computer science teacher to arrange a presentation by an animator, or if you live near an animation studio, try to arrange a tour of a production facility. Sketch as much as you possibly can. Carry a sketchpad around in order to quickly capture images and gestures that seem interesting to you. There are many computer animation software programs available that teach basic principles and techniques. Experiment with these programs to create basic animation. Some video cameras have stop-motion buttons that allow you to take a series of still shots. You can use this feature to experiment with claymation and other stop-motion techniques.

EMPLOYERS

Approximately 87,000 animators and multimedia artists are employed in the United States. Employers of animators include movie studios and television networks. In addition, a number of these artists are self-employed, working on a freelance basis. Some do animation on the Web as a part-time business or a hobby.

Animators are also employed outside the film and television industries by advertising and public relations agencies, the computer and video game industry, and in various computer-related industries.

And the Annie Goes to . . .

The Annie Awards are the animation industry's highest honor. They are presented by the International Animated Film Society, ASIFA-Hollywood. The following animated featured films have won Annies in recent years:

2008: *King Fu Panda*

2007: *Ratatouille*

2006: *Cars*

2005: *Wallace & Gromit in the Curse of the Were-Rabbit*

2004: *The Incredibles*

2003: *Finding Nemo*

2002: *Spirited Away*

2001: *Shrek*

2000: *Toy Story 2*

For more information on animated featured films that have been nominated for or won Annie Awards, visit http://annieawards.org.

One new way up-and-coming animators have made themselves known to the animating community is by attracting an audience on the World Wide Web. A portfolio of well-executed Web 'toons can help an animator build his reputation and get jobs. Some animators, such as the Brothers Chaps (creators of http://homestarrunner.com), have even been able to turn their creations into a profitable business.

STARTING OUT

Aspiring animators should contact animation companies directly for information on job openings. Job listings are also available at AnimationWorldNetwork (http://www.awn.com). College career services offices also provide job listings, and animation professors can often provide valuable industry connections. Participation in an internship will provide aspiring animators with valuable contacts, which could lead to job opportunities.

ADVANCEMENT

Animators' success, like that of other artists, depends on how much the public likes their work. Very successful animators work for well-known film companies and other employers at the best wages; some become well known to the public.

EARNINGS

Multimedia artists and animators employed in the motion picture and video industry earned mean annual salaries of $71,910 in 2008, according to the U.S. Department of Labor. Salaries for all multimedia artists and animators ranged from less than $31,570 to more than $100,390.

Self-employed artists do not receive fringe benefits such as paid vacations, sick leave, health insurance, or pension benefits. Those who are salaried employees of companies and the like do typically receive these fringe benefits.

WORK ENVIRONMENT

Most animators work in large cities where movie and television studios are located. They generally work in well-lit, comfortable environments. Staff animators work a standard 40-hour workweek but may occasionally be expected to work evenings and weekends to meet deadlines. Freelance animators have erratic schedules, and the number of hours they work may depend on how much money they want to earn or how

And the Oscar Goes to . . .

The following animated featured films have won Oscars in recent years:

2008: *WALL-E*

2007: *Ratatouille*

2006: *Happy Feet*

2005: *Wallace & Gromit in the Curse of the Were-Rabbit*

2004: *The Incredibles*

2003: *Finding Nemo*

2002: *Spirited Away*

2001: *Shrek*

For more information on animated featured films that have been nominated for or won Academy Awards, visit http://www.oscars.org/awardsdatabase.

much work they can find. They often work evenings and weekends but are not required to be at work during regular office hours.

Animators can be frustrated by employers who curtail their creativity, asking them to follow instructions that are contrary to what they would most like to do. Many freelance animators spend a lot of time working alone at home, but animators have more opportunities to interact with other people than do most working artists.

OUTLOOK

Employment for animators and multimedia artists is expected to grow much faster than the average for all careers through 2016, according to the U.S. Department of Labor. The growing trend of sophisticated special effects in motion pictures should create opportunities at industry effects houses such as Sony Pictures Imageworks, DreamQuest Software, Blue Sky Studios, Rhythm & Hues Studios, Industrial Light & Magic, and DreamWorks SKG. Furthermore, growing processor and Internet connection speeds are creating excellent opportunities for animators on the Web animation. Demand is also increasing as animation is increasingly used in mobile technologies and in non-entertainment-based fields such as scientific research or design services. Because so many creative and talented people are drawn to this field, however, competition for jobs will be strong.

Animated features are not just for children anymore. Much of the animation today is geared for an adult audience. Interactive computer games, animated films, network and cable television, and the Internet are among the many employment sources for talented animators. More than 60 percent of all visual artists are self-employed, but freelance work can be hard to come by, and many freelancers earn little until they acquire experience and establish a good reputation. Competition for work will be keen; those with an undergraduate or advanced degree in art or film will be in demand. Experience in action drawing and computers is a must.

FOR MORE INFORMATION

For an overview of animation and useful exercises, visit the following Web site:

  Animating: Creating Movement Frame by Frame
  http://www.oscars.org/education-outreach/teachersguide/
    animation/pdf/animation.pdf

For membership and scholarship information, contact
International Animated Film Society-ASIFA Hollywood
2114 West Burbank Boulevard
Burbank, CA 91506-1232
Tel: 818-842-8330
Email: info@asifa-hollywood.org
http://www.asifa-hollywood.org

For an art school directory, a scholarship guide, and general information, contact
National Art Education Association
1916 Association Drive
Reston, VA 20191-1590
Tel: 703-860-8000
Email: info@arteducators.org
http://www.naea-reston.org

For information on this nonprofit society representing visual effects practitioners, visit
Visual Effects Society
5535 Balboa Boulevard, Suite 205
Encino, CA 91316-1544
818-981-7861
info@visualeffectssociety.com
http://www.visualeffectssociety.com

This professional organization is dedicated to the advancement of women in animation. For information, visit
Women in Animation
PO Box 17706
Encino, CA 91416-7706
Email: wia@womeninanimation.org
http://wia.animationblogspot.com/

Business Managers

QUICK FACTS

School Subjects
Art
Business
Computer science
Economics

Personal Skills
Helping/teaching
Leadership/management

Work Environment
Primarily indoors
One location with some
  travel

Minimum Education Level
Bachelor's degree

Salary Range
$45,010 to $130,000 to
  $214,410+

Certification or Licensing
None available

Outlook
Little or no change

DOT
189

GOE
09.01.01, 10.01.01, 13.01.01

NOC
0611

O*NET-SOC
11-1011.00, 11-1011.02,
  11-1021.00, 11-3031.01

OVERVIEW

Business managers plan, organize, direct, and coordinate the operations of companies. They work in the computer and video game industry, the film and television industries, the advertising industry, and many other industries. Business managers may oversee the operations of an entire company, a geographical territory of a company's operations, or a specific department, such as sales and marketing or manufacturing.

HISTORY

Everyone has some experience in management. For example, if you schedule your day so that you can get up, get to school on time, go to soccer practice after school, have the time to do your homework, and get to bed at a reasonable hour, you are practicing management skills. Running a household, paying bills, balancing a checkbook, and keeping track of appointments, meetings, and social activities are also examples of managerial activities. Essentially, the term *manage* means to handle, direct, or control.

Management is a necessary part of any enterprise in which a person or group of people are trying to accomplish a specific goal. In fact, civilization could not have grown to its present level of complexity without the planning and organizing involved in effective management. Some of the earliest examples of written documents had to do with the management of business and commerce. As societies and individuals accumulated property and wealth, they needed effective record keeping of taxes, trade agreements, laws, and rights of ownership.

The technological advances of the industrial revolution brought about the need for a distinct class of managers. As complex factory systems developed, skilled and trained managers were required to organize and operate them. Workers became specialized in a limited number of tasks, which required managers to coordinate and oversee production.

As businesses began to diversify their production, industries became so complex that their management had to be divided among several different managers, as opposed to one central, authoritarian manager. With the expanded scope of managers and the trend toward decentralized management, the transition to the professional manager took place. In the 1920s large corporations began to organize with decentralized administration and centralized policy control.

Managers provided a forum for the exchange and evaluation of creative ideas and technical innovations. Eventually these management concepts spread from manufacturing and production to office, personnel, marketing, and financial functions. Today, management is more concerned with results than activities, taking into account individual differences in styles of working.

Managers play a key role in animation-related industries—from jack-of-all-trades managers at small software publishers and business managers at mom-and-pop animation studios, to the thousands of specialized managers employed by a single major software publisher such as Electronic Arts, Activision Blizzard, or Sony or an animation studio such as Pixar or Rhythm & Hues Studios. They keep projects on schedule, oversee budgets, and ensure that their staff focuses on the big picture—the creation of an entertaining game or an animated feature or commercial.

THE JOB

Business managers direct a company's daily activities within the context of the organization's overall plan. They implement organizational policies and goals. This may involve developing sales or promotional materials (such as creating advertisements or marketing plans for video games such as *Madden NFL* or *Prince of Persia* or an animated feature such as *The Incredibles)*, analyzing the department's budgetary requirements, and hiring, training, and supervising staff (such as animators, game designers, directors, producers, and software engineers). Business managers are often responsible for long-range planning for their company or department. This involves setting goals for the organization and developing a workable plan for meeting those goals. For example, a small video game publisher may set a goal of expanding its business and competing with the larger companies for market share. To do this, managers would need to develop an action plan that would most likely involve hiring more staff, developing more games, improving proprietary software, promoting its existing games, and generally raising its profile in the industry and among game buyers by initiating advertising and marketing campaigns.

A manager responsible for a single department might work to coordinate the department's activities with other departments (such as art direction, marketing, advertising, sound production, etc.). A manager responsible for an entire company or organization might work with the managers of various departments or locations to oversee and coordinate the activities of all departments. If the business is privately owned, the owner may be the manager. In a large corporation, however, there will be a management structure above the business manager.

The hierarchy of managers includes top executives, such as the *president,* who establishes the company's goals and policies along with others, such as the chief executive officer, chief financial officer, chief information officer, executive vice president, and the board of directors. *Top executives* plan business objectives and develop policies to coordinate operations between divisions and departments and establish procedures for attaining objectives. Activity reports and financial statements are reviewed to determine progress and revise operations as needed. The president also directs and formulates funding for new and existing programs within the organization.

Although the president or chief executive officer retains ultimate authority and responsibility, a manager known as a *chief operating officer* or COO oversees the day-to-day operations of the company. Other duties of a COO may include serving as chairman of committees, such as management, executive, design, engineering, or sales.

Some companies have an *executive vice president,* who directs and coordinates the activities of one or more departments, depending on the size of the organization. In very large organizations, the duties of executive vice presidents may be highly specialized. For example, they may oversee the activities of managers of marketing, sales promotion, purchasing, finance, personnel training, production, industrial relations, administrative services, data processing, property management, transportation, or legal services. A vice president of production at a leading game developer such as Activision Blizzard, for example, might have a variety of responsibilities, including providing management and leadership for the production team (two to three senior/executive producers and 10 to 15 producers and associate producers) while overseeing the creation of four to five video games concurrently; interacting with marketing, sales, quality assurance, finance, operations, technology, human resources staff on the development of these titles; and meeting with outside vendors to develop new projects and game lines. In smaller organizations, an executive vice president might be responsible for a number of these departments. Executive vice presidents also assist the chief executive officer in formulating and administering the organization's policies and developing its long-range goals. Executive vice presidents may serve as members of management committees on special studies.

Companies may also have a *chief financial officer* or CFO. In small firms, the CFO is usually responsible for all financial management tasks, such as budgeting, capital expenditure planning, cash flow, and various financial reviews and reports. In larger companies, the CFO may oversee financial management departments, to help other managers develop financial and economic policy and oversee the implementation of these policies.

Satoru Iwata, president and CEO of Nintendo Co. Ltd., speaks at a news conference. *(Ric Francis, AP Photo)*

Chief information officers, or *CIOs,* are responsible for all aspects of their company's information technology. They use their knowledge of technology and business to determine how information technology can best be used to meet company goals. This may include researching, purchasing, and overseeing the set up and use of technology systems, such as intranet, Internet, and computer networks. These managers sometimes take a role in implementing a company's Web site. These managers are especially important in the gaming or television and motion picture animation industries since technology plays such a pivotal role in the creation, design, testing, and marketing of computer and video games and animated films

REQUIREMENTS

High School
The educational background of business managers varies as widely as the nature of their diverse responsibilities. Many have a bachelor's degree in liberal arts or business administration. Those in the gaming industry might also have degrees in game design, computer science, or information technology. Those who work in the film and television industries may have degrees in business, film, production, or other related areas. Your best bet academically is to get a well-rounded education. Because communication is important, take as many English classes as possible. Speech classes are another way to improve your communication skills. Courses in mathematics, business, and computer science are also excellent choices to help you prepare for this career.

Postsecondary Training
Business managers often have a college degree in a subject that pertains to the department they direct or the organization they administer; for example, accounting or economics for a business manager of finance, game design for an art director or design manager, computer science for a business manager of data processing, engineering or science for a director of research and development. As computer usage grows, many managers are expected to have experience with the information technology that applies to their field.

Graduate and professional degrees are common. Many managers in administrative, marketing, financial, and manufacturing activities have a master's degree in business administration. Managers in highly technical manufacturing and research activities often have a master's degree or doctorate in a technical or scientific discipline. A law degree is mandatory for business managers of corporate legal departments.

Other Requirements

There are a number of personal characteristics that help one be a successful business manager, depending upon the specific responsibilities of the position. A manager who oversees other employees should have good communication and interpersonal skills. The ability to delegate work is another important personality trait of a good manager. The ability to think on your feet is often key in business management. Organization is also important, since managers often manage several different games or animated features simultaneously. Other traits considered important for top executives are intelligence, decisiveness, intuition, creativity, honesty, loyalty, a sense of responsibility, and planning abilities. Finally, the successful manager should be flexible and interested in staying abreast of new developments in the industry (for example, new computer technology that allows games to become more entertaining and user-friendly or films to incorporate more computer-generated imagery).

EXPLORING

To get experience as a manager, start with your own interests. Whether you're involved in drama, sports, school publications, or a part-time job, there are managerial duties associated with any organized activity. These can involve planning, scheduling, managing other workers or volunteers, fund-raising, or budgeting. Local businesses also have job opportunities through which you can get firsthand knowledge and experience of management structure. If you can't get an actual job, at least try to schedule a meeting with a business manager to talk about the career. Some schools or community organizations arrange job shadowing, where you can spend part of a day "shadowing" a selected employee to see what the job is like. Joining Junior Achievement (http://www.ja.org) is another excellent way to get involved with local businesses and learn about how they work. Finally, take every opportunity to work with computers, since computer skills are vital to today's business world. If you are interested in working in the gaming industry, for example, learn as much as you can about computer and video games and the industry as a whole. If you are interested in working in the motion picture industry, learn as much as you can about the major animation studios and industry associations. Read industry trade publications and visit the Web sites of professional associations (see For More Information).

EMPLOYERS

All animation-related companies have some form of managerial positions. Obviously, the larger the company is, the more managerial positions it is likely to have. Another factor is the geographical territory covered by the business. It is safe to say that companies doing business in larger geographical territories are likely to have more managerial positions than those with smaller territories. Major entertainment software publishers include Electronic Arts, Nintendo of America, Atari, Sony, Activision Blizzard, THQ, Take-Two Interactive, Microsoft, and Konami Digital Entertainment-America. In addition to these large companies, there are many small-to-mid-level software publishers. Large animation companies include Pixar, Lucasfilm Animation, Blue Sky Studios, Rhythm & Hues Studios, Walt Disney Animation Studios, Warner Bros. Animation Studios, Sony Pictures Animation, and DreamWorks Animation SKG. Visit http://aidb.com for a database of thousands of animation-related companies.

STARTING OUT

Your college career services office is often the best place to start looking for jobs. A number of listings can also be found in newspaper help wanted ads. If you are interested in working in the gaming industry, the Internet is a good resource. Web sites such as Animation World Network (http://www.awn.com), HighendCareers (http://www.highendcareers.com), GameJobs (http://www.gamejobs.com), Gamasutra (http://www.gamasutra.com), and Dice (http://www.dice.com) provide information on jobs and employers. You might also enter the field by participating in an internship at a software developer during your college years or networking with gaming professionals at industry conferences such as the Game Developers Conference (http://www.gdconf.com).

If you are interested in working for animation studios, the aforementioned Web sites will provide job listings. You should also contact employers directly to investigate job leads. Many organizations have management trainee programs that college graduates can enter. Such programs are advertised at college career fairs or through college career services offices. Often, however, these management trainee positions are filled by employees who are already working for the organization and who demonstrate management potential.

ADVANCEMENT

Most business management and top executive positions are filled by experienced lower-level managers and executives who display valuable managerial traits, such as leadership, self-confidence, creativity, motivation, decisiveness, and flexibility. In small firms advancement to a higher management position may come slowly, while promotions may occur more quickly in larger firms.

Advancement may be accelerated by participating in different kinds of educational programs available for managers. These are often paid for by the organization. Company training programs broaden knowledge of company policy and operations. Training programs sponsored by industry and trade associations and continuing education courses in colleges and universities can familiarize managers with the latest developments in management techniques. In recent years, large numbers of middle managers were laid off as companies streamlined operations. Competition for jobs is keen, and business managers committed to improving their knowledge of the field and of related disciplines—especially computer information systems—will have the best opportunities for advancement.

Business managers may advance to executive or administrative vice president. Vice presidents may advance to peak corporate positions—president or chief executive officer. Presidents and chief executive officers, upon retirement, may become members of the board of directors of one or more firms. Sometimes business managers establish their own firms.

EARNINGS

Salary levels for business managers vary substantially, depending upon the level of responsibility, length of service, and type, size, and location of the company. Top-level managers at large software publishers and animation companies can earn much more than their counterparts at small companies. Also, salaries in large metropolitan areas, such as New York City and Los Angeles, where a large number of software publishers and animation companies are located, are higher than those in smaller cities.

The U.S. Department of Labor reports that general and operations managers employed in all industries had a median yearly income of $91,570 in 2008. Salaries ranged from less than $45,010 to $137,020 or more. Chief executives earned a mean annual salary of $158,560 in 2008. Those employed in the film and television industries earned mean annual salaries of $214,410.

Game Developer magazine reports that business professionals in the computer and video game industry earned approximately $102,143 in 2008. Experienced vice-presidents and executive managers with at least six years of experience averaged $131,085.

Benefit and compensation packages for business managers are usually excellent, and may even include such things as bonuses, stock awards, company-paid insurance premiums, use of company cars, paid country club memberships, expense accounts, and generous retirement benefits.

WORK ENVIRONMENT

Business managers are provided with comfortable offices near the departments they direct. Top executives may have spacious, lavish offices and may enjoy such privileges as executive dining rooms, company cars, country club memberships, and liberal expense accounts.

Managers often travel between national, regional, and local offices. Top executives may travel to meet with executives in other corporations, both within the United States and abroad. Meetings and conferences sponsored by industries and associations occur regularly and provide invaluable opportunities to meet with peers and keep up with the latest developments. In large corporations, job transfers between the parent company and its local offices or subsidiaries are common.

Business managers often work long hours under intense pressure to meet, for example, production and marketing goals. Some executives spend up to 80 hours working each week. These long hours limit time available for family and leisure activities.

OUTLOOK

Overall, employment of business managers and executives employed in all industries is expected to experience little or no growth through 2016, according to the U.S. Department of Labor. Some job openings will occur as a result of managers being promoted to better positions, retiring, or leaving their positions to start their own businesses. Even so, the compensation and prestige of these positions make them highly sought after, and competition to fill openings will be intense.

Employment for top executives in the motion picture and video industries is expected to change little through 2016.

Business managers employed in the computer and video game industry should have better employment prospects. The industry has enjoyed strong sales in the last decade, and managers will be needed as companies expand and add new product lines.

Business managers who have knowledge of one or more foreign languages (such as Spanish or Mandarin) and experience in marketing, international economics, and information systems will have the best employment opportunities.

FOR MORE INFORMATION

For industry information, contact
 Academy of Interactive Arts and Sciences
 23622 Calabasas Road, Suite 220
 Calabasas, CA 91302-4111
 Tel: 818-876-0826
 http://www.interactive.org

For news about management trends, resources on career information and finding a job, and an online job bank, contact
 American Management Association
 1601 Broadway
 New York, NY 10019-7434
 Tel: 877-566-9441
 http://www.amanet.org

For industry information, contact
 Entertainment Software Association
 575 Seventh Street, NW, Suite 300
 Washington, DC 20004-1611
 Email: esa@theesa.com
 http://www.theesa.com

For comprehensive career information, including the resource "Breaking In: Preparing For Your Career in Games," visit the IGDA Web site.
 International Game Developers Association (IGDA)
 19 Mantua Road
 Mt. Royal, NJ 08061-1006
 Tel: 856-423-2990
 http://www.igda.org

For information on management careers, contact
 National Management Association
 2210 Arbor Boulevard
 Dayton, OH 45439-1506
 Tel: 937-294-0421
 Email: nma@nma1.org
 http://nma1.org

College Professors, Animation

QUICK FACTS

School Subjects
Art
Computer science
Speech

Personal Skills
Communication/ideas
Helping/teaching

Work Environment
Primarily indoors
Primarily one location

Minimum Education Level
Master's degree

Salary Range
$35,320 to $66,640 to
$124,430+

Certification or Licensing
None available

Outlook
Much faster than the average

DOT
090

GOE
12.03.02

NOC
4121

O*NET-SOC
25-1021.00

OVERVIEW

Animation professors instruct undergraduate and graduate students in animation-related subjects at colleges and universities. They are responsible for teaching students about animation techniques, game programming, computer graphics, game physics, 3D modeling and animation, scriptwriting, sound production, game design and level design, and other related subjects. They also may conduct research, write for publication, and aid in administration.

HISTORY

The concept of colleges and universities goes back many centuries. These institutions evolved slowly from monastery schools, which trained a select few for certain professions, notably theology. The terms *college* and *university* have become virtually interchangeable in America outside the walls of academia, although originally they designated two very different kinds of institutions.

Two of the most notable early European universities were the University of Bologna in Italy, thought to have been established in the 12th century, and the University of Paris, which was chartered in 1201. These universities were considered to be models after which other European universities were patterned. Oxford University in England was probably established during the 12th century. Oxford served as a model for early American colleges and universities and today is still considered one of the world's leading institutions.

Harvard, the first U.S. college, was established in 1636. Its stated purpose was to train men for the ministry; the early colleges were all established for religious training. With the growth of state-supported institutions in the early 18th century, the process of freeing the curriculum from ties with the church began. The University of Virginia established the first liberal arts curriculum in 1825, and these innovations were later adopted by many other colleges and universities.

Although the original colleges in the United States were patterned after Oxford University, they later came under the influence of German universities. During the 19th century, more than 9,000 Americans went to Germany to study. The emphasis in German universities was on the scientific method. Most of the people who had studied in Germany returned to the United States to teach in universities, bringing this objective, factual approach to education and to other fields of learning.

In 1833 Oberlin College in Oberlin, Ohio, became the first college founded as a coeducational institution. In 1836 the first women-only college, Wesleyan Female College, was founded in Macon, Georgia.

The junior college movement in the United States has been one of the most rapidly growing educational developments. Junior colleges first came into being just after the turn of the 20th century.

Early animators in the United States were largely self-taught. Others took basic drawing classes at art schools and then applied these skills toward work in the animation industry. The first film school in the United States was founded in 1929 at the University of Southern California (USC), but animation-related courses were not part of its early curricula.

In the early 1930s Walt Disney actually drove some of his employees to the Chouinard Institute, an art school in Los Angeles, to improve their drawing skills, according to "Walt's Jalopy: Animator Training through the Decades," an article in *Animation World* magazine by Tom Sito. Disney also brought teachers from the institute to his studio to teach his staff on site. Sito reports that by 1941 Disney was spending $100,000 a year for these classes. While some scoffed at this expense, Sito says that these classes helped the "overall quality of the studio's work grow by leaps and bounds." In 1942 a Disney animator taught "The Principles and Mechanics of Animation" at USC. It is considered to be one of the first formal animation classes offered in the United States. After World War II, colleges and universities began offering animation classes and programs. In 1946 a Disney animator started an animation course at the University of California

Tips on Submitting a Demo Reel

Fifty percent of animators surveyed by AnimationMentor.com say that "creating a high-quality demo reel" is the most important step to landing a job in the field, according to AnimationMentor.com. A demo reel features examples of your work that will demonstrate your animation style, skill, and creativity to potential employers. Here are some tips to keep in mind when preparing your demo reel.

- **Keep your reel to four minutes or less.** Think of a four-minute demo reel as the equivalent of a two-page resume—the absolute longest you would ever make this document. Hiring managers must view hundreds or even thousands of reels, and they won't have time to sit through your 10-minute reel waiting for your best work.

- **Don't string a bunch of unrelated clips together.** It will just confuse viewers. For example, present an entire two-minute animation, not just a portion. Then follow this up with another full-length animation.

- **Be careful using sound.** Hiring managers either turn off sound when viewing a reel or, if they do listen, profess to being annoyed if it's a bad match for the animation or just poorly done. Remember, animation studios have professionals on staff to create music and other sounds, so they won't need your musical talents.

- **Provide a demo reel breakdown.** Detail what the reel will show: the type of animation, what you did to create the animation, and the software or other technology you used to create it.

- **Ask your friends and fellow animation students to view your reel before submission.** They can provide feedback on your presentation, the actual animation, effective use of color, and other features.

- **Take the time to make it look great.** It is tempting to rush to send out your demo reel when you hear about a great job lead, but sending an unfinished or unpolished reel will reduce your chances of getting hired in this highly competitive industry.

Source: Pixar

in Los Angeles (UCLA). This eventually became known as the UCLA Animation Workshop, which is still educating students today. Many animation schools were founded in the ensuing years—some of which helped aspiring animators develop more personal, nontraditional techniques and approaches. Today, animation courses and majors (including those that focus on animation techniques for computer and video games) are available at hundreds of colleges and universities throughout the United States. In 1994 DigiPen Institute of Technology in Redmond, Washington, became the first postsecondary institution in North America to offer a two-year degree in game programming.

THE JOB

Animation faculty members teach at junior colleges or at four-year colleges and universities. At four-year institutions, most faculty members are *assistant professors, associate professors,* or *full professors.* These three types of professorships differ in regard to status, job responsibilities, and salary. Assistant professors are new faculty members who are working to get tenure (status as a permanent professor); they seek to advance to associate and then to full professorships.

Animation professors perform three main functions: teaching, advising, and research. Their most important responsibility is to teach students. Their role within the department will determine the level of courses they teach and the number of courses per semester. Most professors work with students at all levels, from college freshmen to graduate students. They may head several classes a semester or only a few a year. Though professors may spend fewer than 10 hours a week in the actual classroom, they spend many hours preparing lesson plans, grading assignments and exams, and preparing grade reports. They also schedule office or computer laboratory hours during the week to be available to students outside of regular classes, and they meet with students individually throughout the semester. In the classroom, professors lecture about animation and game design theory and other topics; demonstrate animation techniques and software (such as Flash, Maya, C++, and Java); lead discussions about screenwriting, music composition, character and environment modeling, and other topics; administer exams; and assign textbook reading and other research. While most professors teach entry-level animation classes such as "Introduction to Computer Gaming" "Introduction to Film Animation," or "Game Development 101," some also teach higher-level classes that center on a particular specialty. For a computer graphics class, for example, professors may teach students how to create computerized animations or digital illustrations. In some courses, game design professors rely heavily on computer laboratories to teach course material.

Another important responsibility is advising students. Not all faculty members serve as advisers, but those who do must set aside large blocks of time to guide students through the program. College professors who serve as advisers may have any number of students assigned to them, from fewer than 10 to more than 100, depending on the administrative policies of the college. Their responsibility may involve looking over a planned program of studies to make sure the students meet requirements for graduation, or it may involve working intensively with each student on many aspects of college life. They may also discuss the different fields of animation (such as computer gaming or animated features) with students and help them identify the best career choices.

The third responsibility of college and university faculty members is research and publication. Faculty members who are heavily involved in research programs sometimes are assigned a smaller teaching load. College animation professors publish their research findings in various scholarly journals such *Animation Journal, Computer Graphics World, Animation Magazine,* or *CARTOON* or in gaming industry publications such as *Game Developer* and *GameInformer.* They also write books based on their research or on their own knowledge and experience in the field. Most textbooks are written by college and university teachers, or veterans of the computer or animation industries. Publishing a significant amount of work—and helping design popular computer and video games or creating animated films—has been the traditional standard by which assistant animation professors prove themselves worthy of becoming permanent, tenured faculty. Typically, pressure to publish is greatest for assistant professors. Pressure to publish increases again if an associate professor wishes to be considered for a promotion to full professorship.

Some faculty members eventually rise to the position of *department chair,* where they govern the affairs of an entire computer gaming, film, or animation department. Department chairs, faculty, and other professional staff members are aided in their myriad duties by *graduate assistants,* who may help develop teaching materials, moderate computer laboratories, conduct research, give examinations, teach lower-level courses, and carry out other activities.

REQUIREMENTS

High School

Your high school's college preparatory program likely includes courses in computer science, English, science, foreign language, history, and mathematics. In addition, you should take courses in speech to get a sense of what it will be like to lecture to a group of students. Your school's debate team can also help you develop public speaking skills, along with research skills. Your high school may

A professor and graduate student (*right*) look at a version of the computer game *Urban Science*, which allows middle school students to try their hand at planning the downtown area of Madison, Wisconsin. *(The Capital Times, Henry Koshollek, AP Photo)*

even offer introductory courses in computer gaming or animation. If so, take as many of these as possible.

Postsecondary Training

At least one advanced degree in computer and video game design, computer animation, film animation, computer science, computer engineering, information management, information technology, or another computer field is required to be an animation professor at a college or university. The master's degree is considered the minimum standard, and graduate work beyond the master's is usually desirable. If you hope to advance in academic rank above instructor, most institutions require a doctorate. Many large universities and colleges have a strong preference for those with a Ph.D. in computer science, information management, or a closely related field.

In the last year of your undergraduate program, you'll apply to graduate programs in your area of study. Standards for admission to a graduate program can be high and the competition heavy, depending on the school. Once accepted into a program, your responsibilities will be similar to those of your professors—in addition to attending seminars, you'll research, prepare articles for publication, and teach some undergraduate courses.

You may find employment in a junior college with only a master's degree. Advancement in responsibility and in salary, however, is more likely to come if you have earned a doctorate.

Other Requirements

You should definitely like working with computers, animation, and computer games, but also enjoy reading, writing, and researching. Not only will you spend many years studying in school, but your whole career will be based on communicating your thoughts and ideas, as well as abstract concepts to students. People skills are important because you'll be dealing directly with students, administrators, and other faculty members on a daily basis. You should feel comfortable in a role of authority and possess self-confidence.

EXPLORING

Learn as much as you can about animation, computer hardware, computer software, and the Internet. Visit Web sites and read books and magazines that relate to computers, animation, the film and television industries, and the gaming industry. Join a computer or gaming club at your school.

Your high school computer science and computer gaming teachers use many of the same skills as college professors, so talk to your teachers about their careers and their college experiences. You can develop your own teaching experience by volunteering at a community center, working at a day care center, or working at a summer camp. Also, spend some time on a college campus to get a sense of the environment. Write to colleges for their admissions brochures and course catalogs (or check them out online); read about the faculty members and the courses they teach. Before visiting college campuses, make arrangements to speak to professors who teach courses that interest you. These professors may allow you to sit in on their classes or labs and observe. Also, make appointments with college advisers and with people in the admissions and recruitment offices. If your grades are good enough, you might be able to serve as a teaching assistant during your undergraduate years, which can give you experience leading discussions and grading papers.

EMPLOYERS

Animation professors teach in undergraduate and graduate programs. The teaching jobs at doctoral institutions are usually better paying and more prestigious. The most sought-after positions are those that offer tenure. Teachers who have only a master's degree will be limited to opportunities with junior colleges, community colleges, and some small private institutions.

Hundreds of colleges and universities across the United States offer courses and degree programs in animation, game design, and related subjects. The International Game Developers Association offers a list of schools at its Web site (http://archives.igda.org/breakingin/resource_schools.php). You can also locate film-related programs by visiting the College Navigator Web site (http://nces.ed.gov/collegenavigator), which is sponsored by the National Center for Education Statistics.

STARTING OUT

You should start the process of finding a teaching position while you are in graduate school. The process includes developing a curriculum vitae (a detailed, academic resume), writing for publication, assisting with research, attending conferences, and gaining teaching experience and recommendations. Many students begin applying for teaching positions while finishing their graduate program. For most positions at four-year institutions, you must travel to large conferences where interviews can be arranged with representatives from the universities to which you have applied.

Because of the competition for tenure-track positions, you may have to work for a few years in temporary positions, visiting various schools as an *adjunct professor*. Some professional associations maintain lists of teaching opportunities in their areas. They may also make lists of applicants available to college administrators looking to fill an available position.

There are also many Web sites that list positions for educators, including Animation World Network (http://www.awn.com), HighendCareers (http://www.highendcareers.com), GameJobs (http://www.gamejobs.com), Gamasutra (http://www.gamasutra.com), and Dice (http://www.dice.com). *The Chronicle of Higher Education* is a weekly resource that covers developments in the education industry. It offers a comprehensive list of job openings for college teachers in its print and online (http://chronicle.com/jobs) editions.

Some professors begin teaching after having successful careers in the computer or gaming industry, creating animated feature films or televisions shows, or by working in the advertising industry on animation-related projects.

ADVANCEMENT

The normal pattern of advancement is from instructor to assistant professor, to associate professor, to full professor. All four academic ranks are concerned primarily with teaching and research. College faculty members who have an interest in and a talent for administration may advance to department chair or dean of their college. A few become college or university presidents or other types of administrators.

The instructor is usually an inexperienced college teacher who may hold a doctorate or may have completed all the Ph.D. requirements except for the dissertation. Most colleges look upon the rank of instructor as the period during which the college is trying out the teacher. Instructors usually are advanced to the position of assistant professors within three to four years. Assistant professors are given up to about six years to prove themselves worthy of tenure, and if they do so, they become associate professors. Some professors choose to remain at the associate level. Others strive to become full professors and receive greater status, salary, and responsibilities.

Most colleges have clearly defined promotion policies from rank to rank for faculty members, and many have written statements about the number of years in which instructors and assistant professors may remain in grade. Administrators in many colleges hope to encourage younger faculty members to increase their skills and competencies and thus to qualify for the more responsible positions of associate professor and full professor.

EARNINGS

According to the U.S. Department of Labor, in 2008 the median salary for computer science postsecondary instructors (a category that includes animation professors) was $66,640, with 10 percent earning $124,430 or more and 10 percent earning $35,320 or less. Those with the highest earnings tend to be senior tenured faculty; those with the lowest, graduate assistants. Professors working on the West Coast and the East Coast and those working at doctorate-granting institutions also tend to earn the highest salaries. Many professors try to increase their earnings by completing research, working as freelancers in animation-related industries, publishing in their field, or teaching additional courses.

Benefits for full-time faculty typically include health insurance and retirement funds and, in some cases, stipends for travel related to research, housing allowances, and tuition waivers for dependents.

WORK ENVIRONMENT

A college or university is usually a pleasant place in which to work. Campuses bustle with all types of activities and events, stimulating ideas, and a young, energetic population. Much prestige comes with success as a professor and scholar; professors have the respect of students, colleagues, and others in their community.

Depending on the size of the department, animation professors may have their own offices, or they may have to share an office with one or more colleagues. Their department may provide them with research assistants to assist them in their work. College professors are also able to do much of their office work at home. They can arrange their schedule around class hours, academic meetings, and the established office hours when they meet with students. Most teachers work more than 40 hours each week. Although animation professors may teach only two or three classes a semester, they spend many hours preparing for lectures and computer labs, examining student work, and conducting research.

OUTLOOK

The U.S. Department of Labor predicts that employment for all college and university professors is expected to grow much faster than the average for all careers through 2016. College enrollment is projected to grow due to an increased number of 18 to 24 year olds, an increased number of adults returning to college, and an increased number of foreign-born students. Retirement of current faculty members will also provide job openings. However, competition for full-time, tenure-track positions at four-year schools will be very strong.

Employment for computer science professors (including those who teach animation-related courses) should also be strong. A growing number of colleges and universities are creating game design programs or adding game design classes in response to student interest. New creative outlets for animated features—such as the Internet, mobile phones, and MP3 players—have created strong demand for new animated films and shorts. Animators will be needed to create these works, and animation professors will be in demand to teach aspiring animators skills that will help them stand out in this competitive market.

FOR MORE INFORMATION

To read about the issues affecting college professors, contact the following organizations:

American Association of University Professors
1133 19th Street, NW, Suite 200
Washington, DC 20036-3655
Tel: 202-737-5900
Email: aaup@aaup.org
http://www.aaup.org

American Federation of Teachers
555 New Jersey Avenue, NW
Washington, DC 20001-2029
Tel: 202-879-4400
Email: online@aft.org
http://www.aft.org

For industry information, contact
Entertainment Software Association
575 Seventh Street, NW, Suite 300
Washington, DC 20004-1611
Email: esa@theesa.com
http://www.theesa.com

For comprehensive career information, including "Breaking In: Preparing For Your Career in Games," visit the association's Web site.
International Game Developers Association
19 Mantua Road
Mt. Royal, NJ 08061-1006
Tel: 856-423-2990
http://www.igda.org

This nonprofit organization represents "visual effects practitioners including artists, technologists, model makers, educators, studio leaders, supervisors, public relations/marketing specialists, and producers in all areas of entertainment from film, television and commercials to music videos and games." Visit its Web site for information about festivals and presentations and news about the industry.
Visual Effects Society
5535 Balboa Boulevard, Suite 205
Encino, CA 91316-1544
Tel: 818-981-7861
Email: info@visualeffectssociety.com
http://www.visualeffectssociety.com

Computer and Video Game Artists and Animators

OVERVIEW

Computer and video game artists and *animators* use their computer skills as well as their artistic abilities to produce games that may entertain, test, and even teach players. Artists and animators work as part of a team that develops a concept for a game, the game rules, the various levels of play, and the game story from beginning to end. Depending on the size of the company they work for and the project they are working on, artists and animators may be responsible for working on one specific game aspect, such as *texture* (that is, creating the textured look for each object in the game), or be responsible for working on several game aspects, such as character building, environment, and motion.

HISTORY

The computer video gaming industry is a relatively new field that can trace its roots back to the second half of the 20th century. At that time, computers were still very large machines that were expensive to run and available only in such places as universities and government research laboratories. While a number of people created forerunners to computer video games, the first such game was not developed until several students at the Massachusetts Institute of Technology began working on the idea. In 1962 their efforts resulted in *Spacewar*, the first

Books to Read

Beck, Jerry. *The Animated Movie Guide*. Chicago: Chicago Review Press, 2005.

Bendazzi, Giannalberto. *Cartoons: One Hundred Years of Cinema Animation*. Bloomington, Ind.: Indiana University Press, 1995.

Gabler, Neal. *Walt Disney: The Triumph of the American Imagination*. New York: Vintage Books, 2007.

Hauser, Tim. *The Art of WALL-E*. San Francisco: Chronicle Books, 2008.

Johnston, Ollie, and Frank Thomas. *The Illusion of Life: Disney Animation*. New York: Disney Editions, 1995.

Kushner, David. *Masters of Doom: How Two Guys Created an Empire and Transformed Pop Culture*. New York: Random House, 2004.

Loguidice, Bill, and Matt Barton. *Vintage Games: An Insider Look at the History of Grand Theft Auto, Super Mario, and the Most Influential Games of All Time*. St. Louis, Mo.: Focal Press, 2009.

Price, David A. *The Pixar Touch*. New York: Vintage Books, 2009.

Whalen, Zach, and Laurie N. Taylor. *Playing the Past: History and Nostalgia in Video Games*. Nashville, Tenn.: Vanderbilt University Press, 2008.

fully interactive game specifically made to be played on a computer. Steve Russell was the main programmer of *Spacewar* and is considered one of the founders of this field. In 1966 Ralph Baer, an engineer and inventor, created his own video game and game console based on a television set. He continued to work on his invention, which became commercially available as *The Odyssey* in 1972. In addition to Russell and Baer, inventor Nolan Bushnell was instrumental in creating the computer video game industry. While Baer was working on game equipment to be used in the home, Bushnell focused his efforts on arcades, where he thought video games could become commercially successful. His game *Computer Space* was the first video game designed to be played in an arcade. However, the game proved too complicated to operate and it did not become popular. Nevertheless, Bushnell continued his game work, and in 1972 he and programmer Al Alcorn created *Pong*. *Pong* was a simple video game of tennis that became wildly popular and revolutionized the industry.

Once people had caught on to the easy yet addictively fun game of *Pong*, they were willing to try out other video games and wanted more variety. As game creators worked on developing new games, they improved existing technologies and invented new ones to enhance their work. The development and popularization of equipment, such as home game consoles, personal computers, the Internet, and mobile phones, also meant games could be played in a wide variety of places and at just about any time. And as computer technologies grew ever more sophisticated, the artistic quality of games also improved. Colors, textures, smooth movement, sounds, and multiple levels of play are just some of the game features that have improved over the years and will continue to do so. As games have become more complex and the industry grown, workers have begun to specialize in areas that interest them, such as programming, testing, and artistic quality. Today's game artists and animators are skilled professionals responsible for the look of everything a game player sees on the screen.

THE JOB

Game artists and animators work on the creation of games, which can fall into several categories, including sports, action/adventure, simulation, and education. Today, games are also played in a variety of environments, such as on personal computers, in arcades, over the Internet, on cell phones, and on consoles at home. Additionally, games are typically created to appeal to a certain audience, for example, boys, girls, teens, men in their 20s, or everyone. As they do their work, artists and animators must always keep these factors in mind to ensure that the look they produce will meet the game's requirements.

Artists and animators may work at small, start-up companies that are trying to produce their first big-hit game, or they may work at established companies, producing new games for an already successful series. Because of factors such as company size, personal skills and experience, type of game worked on, and developing technologies, not all game artists and animators have the same responsibilities—or even the same job titles—throughout the industry. Some may specialize on a particular aspect of the game, such as creating the game's environments (for example, a forest, a city, the surface of another planet), while others may work on multiple aspects of a game, such as building a character, animating it, and creating other objects in the game. No matter what their job title or the type of game they work on, however, artists and animators must be able to work as part of a team because several groups, or teams, of people usually work together to produce a game. In addition to the artists and animators, these include people who come up with the game idea and its rules, computer programmers who create the software for the game, and game testers who make sure the game works properly.

Game designers begin the process of developing a video game by considering the intended audience, the type of equipment on which the game will be played, and the number of players to be involved. They collaborate to come up with a workable game idea, game rules, and levels of play. *Conceptual artists* sometimes create storyboards, which sketch out elements of the game, such as characters and action, and set a visual tone that the final product should have. This sketch work does not typically become part of the finished product's "in-game" art. It does, though, give the other artists a visual direction on which to base their work.

Video games are made to look two-dimensional (2D), three-dimensional (3D), or combine both 2D and 3D features. Artists who create in-game art with a 2D look do this by drawing on paper then scanning the work into a computer. Artists who create in-game art that has a 3D look use special computer software to make the artwork inside a computer. Some artists may also build models or sculptures of objects then use a 3D scanner to scan the model into the computer. The artist may then use software to touch up the image until it has the desired look.

Character artists, also called *character builders*, are responsible for creating the characters in a game. They may draw a variety of sketches to plan out the character whether it is 2D or 3D. Then, to create a 3D character, character artists work on a computer and begin building the character from the inside out. To do this, they use software that generates basic shapes, which they manipulate to create a "skeleton" for the character. The artists then add skin, fur, scales or other types of covering to the skeleton as well as colors and details, such as the eyes.

Background artists, sometimes known as *environmental modelers* or *modelers,* create the game's settings. For example, they may need to create realistic city scenes with various buildings, parking ramps, and streets for different levels of play in the game. They may also need to build backgrounds for imaginary places, such as a planet in another galaxy. Background artists are responsible for providing the right setting for the game, and they must make sure their artwork is in correct proportion to other game elements. To do this for 3D environments, they sketch out their designs on paper, consult with other artists, and use the computer to build the backgrounds. In some cases, the background artist will create objects that are part of the scene, such as the furniture in a room, or items a character might use, like a sword or magic stone. In other cases, another artist—a *3D object specialist* or *object builder*—will create such items. Once again, this artist must make sure his or her work is in proportion to the other artwork and matches the game's visual style.

Texture artists add detail to all the game's artwork so that the surface of each element appears as it should. Texture artists, for example, make a brick wall in a background look rough and brick-like, make a character in the rain look wet, or make a treasure of jewels sparkle and shine. They work fairly closely with the background artists to ensure that the textures they create match what those artists had envisioned. To build textures, texture artists may draw, paint, or photograph surfaces then scan the images into the computer. They use software to manipulate the texture image and "wrap" it around the object on which they are working.

Animators are responsible for giving movement to the game's characters. They must have an understanding of human anatomy and often model game characters' movements on actual human or animal movement. After all, even if the character is a green, three-eyed alien with wings, it still needs to move smoothly and believably through a scene. In one method of animation, the artist builds a model or sculpture of a character, scans it into the computer, and then uses software to animate the character in the computer. In another method, which is typically used with sports games to create the realistic movements of athletes, actual people are used as models. In this method, called "motion capture," a person wearing body sensors goes through whatever motions the game character will be doing—jumping, throwing a football, running, dribbling a basketball, and so on. The motion sensors send information to a computer and the computer creates a "skeleton" of the person in motion. The animator then builds on this skeleton, adding skin, clothing, and other details.

Animators are also responsible for getting characters' personalities to show through. They must use their artistic skills to convey feelings, such as anger, fear, and happiness, through a character's facial expressions and body language. Animators may work closely with the character artists and the game designers to get an understanding of each character's personality and goals. That way animators can determine, for example, if a character's smile should be wide and friendly, small and meek, or more like a sneer than a real smile.

All artists and animators must keep practical information in mind as they do their work. The type of equipment a game is designed for,

for example, will impose limitations on such elements as the speed of play and the details that will be visible. Artists and animators must also be able to work on schedule, meeting the deadlines set for their stage in the game development process. If an artist comes up with great work but is always missing deadlines, he or she will be delaying the production of the game and perhaps putting the project in jeopardy. Few team members will want to work with someone like that. Additionally, artists and animators need to know how to use available technologies and techniques. Because this work is part of the dynamic computer industry, new equipment and processes are always being developed and refined. Artists and animators must want to keep learning throughout their careers so that their skills are up to date.

REQUIREMENTS

High School

If you are interested in working in the video game field as an artist or animator, you should take art and computer classes in high school. Math classes, such as algebra and geometry, will also be helpful. If your school offers graphic design classes, be sure to take those. Biology classes can offer the opportunity to learn about anatomy and physics can teach you about motion. Most artists and animators today have college degrees, so take classes that will help you prepare for a college education, including history, government, and English.

Postsecondary Training

Many people in this field have degrees in game design, animation, fine arts, graphic arts, or industrial design; but it is possible to enter the field with a degree in another area, such as architecture or computer science. It is important to get a broad-based background in the arts, and traditional arts should not be overlooked. Classes in drawing, sculpture, painting, and color theory will teach you many of the basics artists need to know. Some schools offer classes in animation, and even if you don't plan on becoming an animator, these classes will be helpful to you later in your career. Naturally, computer classes are important to take, and you should try to learn about game art software, such as 3ds Max, as well as other software, like Photoshop. And even though artists and animators usually don't do game programming, take computer programming classes to at least learn the basics. The more you understand about all aspects of game development, the better able you'll be to make your artistic contributions enhance a game.

Other Requirements

Game artists and animators must be creative and able to translate their imaginative ideas into visual representations. They should have a keen sense of color, be able to visualize things in three dimensions, and work as part of a group. Like all artists, they are able to give and receive criticism in a fair and impersonal manner. Curiosity and a willingness to learn are important traits that drive artists and animators to use new technologies or try different techniques to get just the right visual effect for something like a character's shadow. Artists and animators should also like to play games themselves. The enjoyment they get from playing, and an understanding of why they like to play games, helps them to be better game makers.

EXPLORING

If you are interested in becoming a game artist or an animator, you can start quite simply by drawing characters and landscapes. You can try copying images from games that you know or create your own characters and settings. Remember, you don't have to be high-tech right away. It's also important to familiarize yourself with the industry, so read publications such as *Game Developer* (http://www. gdmag.com) and *Animation World* (http://mag.awn.com). You also might want to read the online resource "Breaking In: Preparing for Your Career in Games," which is available at the International Game Developers Association's Web site (http://archives.igda.org/breakingin). The publication offers an overview of visual arts careers, profiles of workers in the field, and other resources. The association also offers student membership. If you have friends who are interested in gaming, try creating your own game or add to a game that exists already. Local museums often offer summer art classes, and community colleges often have computer courses—check these out.

One thing many industry experts recommend is to attend conferences such as SIGGRAPH and the Game Developers Conference, both of which are annual events. There you will be able to meet people in the business and other enthusiasts, see new games and technologies, and even attend workshops of interest to you. This is a terrific opportunity for networking and, if you are in college, you may hear of internship or job opportunities. Of course, this event can be expensive, but if your funds are limited, you may want to work as a student volunteer and pay much less. Information on the conference and volunteer opportunities is available at http://www. gdconf.com. Information on the SIGGRAPH conference is available at http://www.siggraph.org.

EMPLOYERS

Game artists and animators can work at small companies or start-ups whose focus is the development of only one or two games. They can also work at large companies that are involved in the development of many games at once. Major entertainment software publishers include Electronic Arts, Nintendo of America, Atari, Sony, Activision Blizzard, THQ, Take-Two Interactive, Microsoft, and Konami Digital Entertainment-America. In addition, some artists freelance, working with a company for a limited time or on a particular project then moving on to another freelance job with a different company.

STARTING OUT

Artists and animators, whether they are just starting out in the field or experienced professionals applying for a job with a new employer, need to have demo reels that highlight their best work. Potential employers will look at a demo reel to get an idea of the artist's or animator's abilities. Those who are seeking their first job can make a reel using artwork that they have done for school as well as anything they've made on their own. Internships also offer an excellent opportunity to gain hands-on experience, which employers like any new hire to have.

To learn of job openings, college students should network with the teachers in their school program, many of whom have contacts in the industry. Conferences, such as SIGGRAPH and the Game Developers Conference, provide major networking opportunities where students can impress those in the field as well as learn of job openings. The Internet is also a good source to use, and Web sites such as Animation World Network (http://www.awn.com), HighendCareers (http://www.highendcareers.com), GameJobs (http://www.gamejobs.com), Gamasutra (http://www.gamasutra.com), and Dice (http://www.dice.com) offer information on jobs and employers.

ADVANCEMENT

Artists and animators can advance into positions such as *lead artist* and *lead animator*. Their responsibilities can include overseeing the work of a team on a project, going over the artwork of individual members, and keeping the team on their time line. *Art directors* and *animation directors* have even more management responsibilities. They may oversee the work of several teams, assign game projects to teams, plan the time line for a game's development, keep an eye on the budget, and do other administrative tasks. Not all artists and animators want to move into such a position because directors' responsibilities remove them from the hands-on creative process. These artists and animators may choose to advance by continuously upgrading their skills and working in areas of art that they haven't previously tried. With their hard work and broad experience, they can gain a reputation in the industry for the quality and variety of their artwork and become sought-after artists.

EARNINGS

The U.S. Department of Labor does not have specific information on the earnings of game artists and animators. It does, however, provide wage information for multimedia artists and animators, a group that includes those working on computer games. The median annual salary reported for all multimedia artists and animators was $56,330 in 2008, according to the U.S. Department of Labor. The lowest paid 10 percent of this group earned $31,570 or less, while the highest paid 10 percent earned $100,390 or more during the same time period. The International Game Developers Association reports that artists with one to two years of experience earn approximately $57,000.

Artists and animators working for small companies and start-ups may have few if any benefits, such as health insurance and retirement plans. Freelance workers must buy their own health insurance and provide for their retirement themselves. Also, they are not paid during any time off they take for vacations or illnesses. Artists and animators who work for large companies, however, typically receive benefits that include retirement plans, health insurance, and paid vacation and sick days.

WORK ENVIRONMENT

Game artists and animators work primarily indoors and at one location. They work with pens, pencils, and paper as well as with scanners, computers, software, and other high-tech equipment. The environment is usually casual—business suits are not required—but busy and often fast paced. Although artists and animators typically are required to work a 40-hour workweek, there are often times when they will put in much longer hours as they work to fix any problems with a game and complete it on schedule. Because this is a creative environment, artistic disagreements come up from time to time and egos can be involved. These artists and animators, though, also get great satisfaction from their work and appreciate the opportunity to be in an environment where their creativity is valued.

Many of the jobs in this field are located on the East Coast and West Coast, and those just starting out may need to relocate to get employment. In addition, artists and animators frequently move within the industry, from one employer to another. This helps them gain experience as well as work on a variety of projects and advance their careers.

OUTLOOK

The U.S. Department of Labor estimates that employment for multimedia artists and animators will grow much faster than the average for all occupations through 2016. Those within the industry see a bright future as the demand for games continues to grow steadily and technologies make new kinds of games possible. Competition for jobs should be strong since many creative and technically savvy people want to be part of this business.

FOR MORE INFORMATION

For information on animation, contact
Animation World Network
6525 Sunset Boulevard, Garden Suite 10
Hollywood, CA 90028-7212
Tel: 323-606-4200
Email: info@awn.com
http://awn.com

For industry information, contact
Entertainment Software Association
575 Seventh Street, NW, Suite 300
Washington, DC 20004-1611
Email: esa@theesa.com
http://www.theesa.com

For career advice and industry information, contact
International Game Developers Association
19 Mantua Road
Mt. Royal, NJ 08061-1006
Tel: 856-423-2990
http://www.igda.org

Computer and Video Game Designers

OVERVIEW

Computer and video game designers create the ideas and interactivity for games. These games are played on various platforms, or media, such as video consoles and computers, on portable telecommunication devices (such as cell phones), and through online Internet subscriptions. They generate ideas for new game concepts, including sound effects, characters, story lines, and graphics. Designers either work for companies that make the games or create the games on their own and sell their ideas and programs to companies that produce them.

HISTORY

Computer and video game designers are a relatively new breed. The industry did not begin to develop until the 1960s and 1970s, when computer programmers at some large universities, big companies, and government labs began designing games on mainframe computers. Steve Russell was perhaps the first video game designer. In 1962, when he was in college, he made up a simple game called *Spacewar*. Graphics of space ships flew through a starry sky on the video screen, the object of the game being to shoot down enemy ships. Nolan Bushnell, another early designer, played *Spacewar* in college. In 1972 he put the first video game in an arcade; it was a game very much like *Spacewar*, and he called it *Computer Space*. However, many users found the game difficult to play, so it was not a success.

Bruce Artwick published the first of many versions of *Flight Simulator*, and Bushnell later created *Pong*, a game that required the players to paddle electronic ping-pong balls back and forth across the video screen. *Pong* was a big hit, and players spent thousands of quarters in arcade machines all over the country playing it. Bushnell's company, Atari, had to hire more and more designers every week, including Steve Jobs, Alan Kay, and Chris Crawford. These early designers made games with text-based descriptions (that is, no graphics) of scenes and actions with interactivity done through a computer keyboard. Games called *Adventure, Star Trek,* and *Flight Simulator* were among the first that designers created. They used simple commands like "look at building" and "move west." Most games were designed for video machines. Not until the later 1970s did specially equipped TVs and early personal computers (PCs) begin appearing.

In the late 1970s and early 1980s designers working for Atari and Intellivision made games for home video systems, PCs, and video arcades. Many of these new games had graphics, sound, text, and animation. Designers of games like *Pac-Man, Donkey Kong,* and *Space Invaders* were successful and popular. They also started to make role-playing games like the famous *Dungeons and Dragons*. Richard Garriott created *Ultima*, another major role-playing game. Games began to feature the names and photos of their programmers on the packaging, giving credit to individual designers.

Workers at Electronic Arts began to focus on making games for PCs to take advantage of technology that included the computer keyboard, more memory, and floppy disks. They created games like *Carmen Sandiego* and *M.U.L.E.* In the mid- to late 1980s, new technology included more compact floppies, sound cards, and larger memory. Designers also had to create games that would work on more than just one platform—PCs, Apple computers, and 64-bit video game machines.

In the 1990s Electronic Arts started to hire teams of designers instead of "lone wolf" individuals (those who design games from start to finish independently). Larger teams were needed because games became more complex; design teams would include not only programmers but also artists, musicians, writers, and animators. Designers made such breakthroughs as using more entertaining graphics, creating more depth in role-playing games, using virtual reality in sports games, and using more visual realism in racing games and flight simulators. This new breed of designers created games using techniques like Assembly, C, and HyperCard. By 1994 designers began to use CD-ROM technology to its fullest. In only a few months, *Doom* was a hit. Designers of this game gave players the chance to alter it themselves at various levels, including choices of weapons and enemies. *Doom* still has fans worldwide.

The success of shareware (software that is given away to attract users to want to buy more complete software) has influenced the

Most Popular Game Genres, 2007

Video Games

Action: 22.3 percent

Family entertainment: 17.6 percent

Sports: 14.1 percent

Shooter: 12.1 percent

Racing: 8.3 percent

Role-playing: 7.6 percent

Strategy: 4.7 percent

Fighting: 4.5 percent

Adventure: 4.3 percent

Other games/compilations: 2.3 percent

Children's: 1.0 percent

Arcade: 0.5 percent

Flight: 0.7 percent

Computer Games

Strategy: 33.9 percent

Role-playing: 18.8 percent

Family entertainment: 14.3 percent

Shooter: 11.6 percent

Adventure: 5.0 percent

Children's: 3.5 percent

Other games/compilations: 3.0 percent

Action: 2.6 percent

Sports: 2.5 percent

Flight: 2.2 percent

Racing: 1.5 percent

Arcade: 0.9 percent

Source: The NPD Group/Retail Tracking Service

return of smaller groups of designers. Even the lone wolf is coming back, using shareware and better authoring tools such as sound libraries and complex multimedia development environments. Some designers are finding that they work best on their own or in small teams.

What is on the horizon for game designers? More multiplayer games; virtual reality; improved technology in coprocessors, chips, hardware, and sound fonts; and "persistent worlds," where online games are influenced by and evolve from players' actions. These new types of games require that designers know more and more complex code so that games can "react" to their multiple players.

THE JOB

Designing games involves programming code as well as creating stories, graphics, and sound effects. It is a very creative process, requiring imagination and computer and communication skills to develop games that are interactive and entertaining. As mentioned earlier, some game designers work on their own and try to sell their designs to companies that produce and distribute games; others are employees of companies such as Electronic Arts, Nintendo of America, and many others. Whether designers work alone or for a company, their aim is to create games that get players involved. Game players want to have fun, be challenged, and sometimes learn something along the way.

Each game must have a story line as well as graphics and sound that will entertain and engage the players. Story lines are situations that the players will find themselves in and make decisions about. Designers develop a plan for combining the story or concept, music or other sound effects, and graphics. They design rules to make it fun, challenging, or educational, and they create characters for the stories or circumstances, worlds in which these characters live, and problems or situations these characters will face.

One of the first steps is to identify the audience that will be playing the game. How old are the players? What kinds of things are they interested in? What kind of game will it be: action, adventure, "edutainment," role-playing, or sports? And which platform will the game use: video game system (e.g., Nintendo), wireless device, (cell phone, PDA, etc.), computer (e.g., Macintosh), or online (Internet via subscription)?

The next steps are to create a design proposal, a preliminary design, and a final game design. The proposal is a brief summary of what the game involves. The preliminary design goes much further, outlining in more detail what the concept is (the story of the game); how the players get involved; what sound effects, graphics, and other elements will be included (What will the screen look like? What kinds of sound effects should the player hear?); and what productivity tools (such as word processors, database programs, spreadsheet programs, flow-charting programs, and prototyping programs) the designer intends to use to create these elements. Independent designers submit a product idea and design proposal to a publisher along with a cover letter and resume. Employees work as part of a team to create the proposal and design. Teamwork might include brainstorming sessions to come up with ideas, as well as involvement in market research (surveying the players who will be interested in the game).

The final game design details the basic idea, the plot, and every section of the game, including the startup process, all the scenes (such as innings for baseball games and maps for edutainment games), and all the universal elements (such as rules for scoring, names of char-acters, and a sound effect that occurs every time something specific happens). The story, characters, worlds, and maps are documented. The game design also includes details of the logic of the game, its algorithms (the step-by-step procedures for solving the problems the players will encounter), and its rules; the methods the player will use to load the game, start it up, score, win, lose, save, stop, and play again; the graphic design, including storyboards and sample art; and the audio design. The designer might also include marketing ideas and proposed follow-up games.

Designers interact with other workers and technologists involved in the game design project, including programmers, audio engi-neers, artists, and even *asset managers,* who coordinate the col-lecting, engineering, and distribution of physical assets to the *production team* (the people who will actually produce the physi-cal CD-ROM or DVD).

Designers need to understand games and their various forms, think up new ideas, and experiment with and evaluate new designs. They assemble the separate elements (text, art, sound, video) of a game into a complete, interactive form, following through with careful planning and preparation (such as sketching out scripts, storyboards, and design documents). They write an implementation plan and guidelines (How will designers manage the process? How much will it cost to design the game? How long will the guidelines be—five pages? 300?). Finally, they amend designs at every stage, solving problems and answering questions.

Computer and video game designers often keep scrapbooks, notes, and journals of interesting ideas and other bits of information. They collect potential game material and even catalog ideas, videos, movies, pictures, stories, character descriptions, music clips, sound effects, animation sequences, and interface techniques. The average time it takes to design a game, including all the elements and stages just described, can be from about six to 18 months.

REQUIREMENTS

High School

If you like to play video or computer games, you are already familiar with them. You will also need to learn a programming language like C++ or Java, and you'll need a good working knowledge of the hardware platform for which you plan to develop your games (video, computer, online, etc.). In high school, learn as much as you can about computers: how they work, what kinds there are, how to program them, and any languages you can learn. You should also take physics, chemistry, and computer science. Since designers are creative, take courses such as art, literature, and music as well.

Postsecondary Training

Although strictly speaking you don't have to have a college degree to be a game designer, most companies are looking for creative people who also have a degree. Having one represents that you've been actively involved in intense, creative work; that you can work with others and follow through on assignments; and, of course, that you've learned what there is to know about programming, computer architecture (including input devices, processing devices, memory and storage devices, and output devices), and software engineering. Employers want to know that you've had some practical experience in design.

A growing number of schools offer courses or degrees in game design. Animation World Network offers a database of animation schools at its Web site (http://schools.awn.com). Another good source of schools can be found at the International Game Developers Association's Web site (http://archives.igda.org/breakingin/resource_schools.php).

Recommended college courses include programming (including assembly level), computer architecture, software engineering, computer graphics, data structures, algorithms, game design, communication networks, artificial intelligence (AI) and expert systems, interface systems, mathematics, and physics.

Other Requirements

One major requirement for game design is that you must love to play computer games. You need to continually keep up with technology, which changes fast. Although you might not always use them, you need to have a variety of skills, such as writing stories, programming, and designing sound effects.

You must also have vision and the ability to identify your players and anticipate their every move in your game. You'll also have to be able to communicate well with programmers, writers, artists, musicians, electronics engineers, production workers, and others.

You must have the endurance to see a project through from beginning to end and also be able to recognize when a design should be scrapped.

EXPLORING

One of the best ways to learn about game design is to try to develop copies of easy games, such as *Pong* and *Pac-Man*, or try to change a game that has an editor. (Games like *Klik & Play*, *Empire*, and *Doom* allow players to modify them to create new circumstances and settings.)

For high school students interested in finding out more about how video games and animations are produced, the DigiPen Institute of Technology (https://workshops.digipen.edu/workshops/overview) offers summer workshops. Two-week courses are offered throughout the summer, providing hands-on experience and advice on courses to take in high school to prepare yourself for postsecondary training.

Writing your own stories, puzzles, and games helps develop storytelling and problem-solving skills. Magazines such as *Computer Graphics World* (http://www.cgw.com) and *Game Developer* (http://www.gdmag.com) have articles about digital video and high-end imaging and other technical and design information.

The Most Popular Online Game Genres, 2007

Puzzle/board/game show/trivia/card games: 47.0 percent

Action/sports/strategy/role-play games: 16.0 percent

Downloadable games such as *Bejeweled:* 14.0 percent

Other: 12.0 percent

Persistent multiplayer universe games: 11.0 percent

Source: Entertainment Software Association

EMPLOYERS

Software publishers (such as Electronic Arts and Activision Blizzard) are found throughout the country, though most are located in California, New York, Washington, and Illinois. Big media companies such as Disney have also opened interactive entertainment departments. Jobs should be available at these companies as well as with online services and interactive networks, which are growing rapidly. Visit http://aidb.com for a database of thousands of animation-related companies.

Some companies are involved in producing games only for wireless devices or online play; others produce only for computers; others make games for various platforms.

STARTING OUT

There are a couple of ways to begin earning money as a game designer: independently or as an employee of a company. It is more realistic to get any creative job you can in the industry (for example, as an artist, a play tester, a programmer, or a writer) and learn as you go, developing your design skills as you work your way up to the level of designer.

Contact company Web sites and sites that advertise job openings, such as Animation World Network (http://www.awn.com), HighendCareers (http://www.highendcareers. com), GameJobs (http://www.gamejobs.com), Gamasutra (http://www.gamasutra.com), and Dice (http://www.dice.com).

In addition to a professional resume, it is a good idea to have your own Web site, where you can showcase your demos. Make sure you have designed at least one demo or have an impressive portfolio of design ideas and documents.

Other ways to find a job in the industry include going to job fairs (such as the Game Developers Conference, http://www.gdconf.com), where you find recruiters looking for creative people to work at their companies, and checking in with online user groups, which often post jobs on the Internet.

Also consider looking for an internship to prepare for this career. Many software and entertainment companies hire interns for short-term assignments.

ADVANCEMENT

Just as with many jobs, to have better opportunities to advance their position and possibly earn more money, computer and video game designers have to keep up with technology. They must be willing to constantly learn more about design, the industry, and even financial and legal matters involved in development.

Becoming and remaining great at their job may be a career-long endeavor for computer and video game designers, or just a stepping-stone to another area of interactive entertainment. Some designers start out as artists, writers, or programmers, learning enough in these jobs to eventually design. For example, a person entering this career may begin as a 3D animation modeler and work on enough game life cycles to understand what it takes to be a game designer. He or she may decide to specialize in another area, such as sound effects or even budgeting.

Some designers rise to management positions, such as president or vice president of a software publisher. Others write for magazines and books, teach, or establish their own game companies.

EARNINGS

Most development companies spend up to two years designing a game even before any of the mechanics (such as writing final code and drawing final graphics) begin; more complex games take even longer. Companies budget $1 to 3 million for developing just one game. If the game is a success, designers are often rewarded with bonuses. In addition to bonuses or royalties (the percentage of profits designers receive from each game that is sold), designers' salaries are affected by their amount of professional experience, their location in the country, and the size of their employer. *Game Developer* magazine reports that game designers had average salaries of approximately $67,379 in 2008. Game designers with less than three years of experience earned approximately $46,208. Those with three to six years' experience averaged $54,716 annually, and those with more than six years' experience averaged $74,688 per year. Lead designers/creative directors earned higher salaries, ranging from $60,833 for those with three to six years' experience to $98,370 for workers with six or more years of experience in the field. It is important to note that these salaries are averages, and some designers (especially those at the beginning stages of their careers) earn less than these amounts. These figures, however, provide a useful guide for the range of earnings available. Game designers on the West Coast earn salaries that are approximately 12 percent higher than those employed in other parts of the country, according to *Game Developer*.

Any major software publisher will likely provide benefits such as medical insurance, paid vacations, and retirement plans. Designers who are self-employed must provide their own benefits.

WORK ENVIRONMENT

Computer and video game designers work in office settings, whether at a large company or a home studio. At some companies, artists and designers sometimes find themselves working 24 or 48 hours at a time, so the office areas are set up with sleeping couches and other areas where employees can relax. Because the game development industry is competitive, many designers find themselves under a lot of pressure from deadlines, design problems, and budget concerns.

OUTLOOK

Computer and video games are a fast-growing segment of the U.S. entertainment industry. In fact, the Entertainment Software Association reports that sales of computer and video game software reached $9.5 billion in 2007. As the demand for new games, more sophisticated games, and games to be played on new systems grows, more and more companies will hire skilled people to create and perfect these products. Opportunities for game designers, therefore, should be good.

In any case, game development is popular; the Entertainment Software Association estimates that about 36 percent of American heads of households play computer and video games. People in the industry expect more and more integration of interactive entertainment into mainstream society. Online development tools such as engines, graphic and sound libraries, and programming languages such as Java will probably create opportunities for new types of products that can feature game components.

FOR MORE INFORMATION

For industry information, contact
Academy of Interactive Arts and Sciences
23622 Calabasas Road, Suite 220
Calabasas, CA 91302-4111
Tel: 818-876-0826
http://www.interactive.org

For industry information, contact
Entertainment Software Association
575 Seventh Street, NW, Suite 300
Washington, DC 20004-1611
Email: esa@theesa.com
http://www.theesa.com

For comprehensive career information, including "Breaking In: Preparing for Your Career in Games," visit the IGDA Web site.
International Game Developers Association (IGDA)
19 Mantua Road
Mt. Royal, NJ 08061-1006
Tel: 856-423-2990
http://www.igda.org

═══════════════ INTERVIEW ═══════════════

Tyler Sigman is a game designer, game writer, and game director for Big Sandwich Games Inc. He discussed his career with the editors of Careers in Focus: Animation.

Q. Why did you decide to become a game designer?

A. I've always been extremely passionate about playing games as a hobby, but as a teen I really became enamored with creating entertainment as well. Whether I was playing a role-playing game with my friends or a computer game on my trusty Commodore, I was also thinking about how to tweak games and change the rules. Eventually that developed into a full-blown hobby, and throughout college and my early career as an aerospace engineer, I was constantly tinkering with gaming projects on the side. My first published games were three silly, non-collectible card games called *Night of the Ill-Tempered Squirrel, Witch Hunt,* and *Shrimpin,* but before that I had made role-playing games (RPGs), board games, and video game levels. I also wrote fiction.

Eventually I realized that I was more passionate about making games than airplanes, and I knew I needed to do everything I could to support myself with that passion. Truthfully, a big factor was that I was tired of only being able to devote my tired off-hours to game making and writing, and wanted to have a shot at using my "better quality" hours of the day to do what I loved. Although I adore the paper game industry, it's easier to make a living in the digital game industry, so I relegated my board game design to the backseat and went full-force after a video game job. I was self-taught, but signed up for a course at Vancouver Film School, where I met my future boss (he was teaching a Game Mechanics course) and he hired me right after the seven-week class, thanks to my previous experience and portfolio pieces. Although I had the right skills, I hadn't yet done the proper networking to get myself in the door—meeting him was a really fortunate turn of events for me.

Q. **Can you tell us a little bit about Big Sandwich Games? What's a typical day like on the job? What are your typical responsibilities and hours?**

A. Big Sandwich Games is a third-party game developer based in Vancouver, Canada. "Third-party" means we are not owned directly by a game publisher; our business comes from publishers hiring us to make games for them. We are currently working on a Nintendo Wii game called *Sky Pirates of Neo Terra*, which should be released in the first half of next year, along with the Nintendo DS version as well. Also, we have made several iPhone games, including *Timefold* and *Sugar Buzz*. Console development is our specialty, though, and we plan to continue to develop for Wii as well as Xbox 360 and PS3.

As design director, my daily routine changes every day, and that is something I really love. I am also acting as producer on our current Wii title, so that adds some different responsibilities that many designers/writers don't have to deal with (like scheduling and managing people). However, I'll try to describe a "typical" day.

The workday at Big Sandwich Games starts at 10 A.M. Compared to most careers, that is really late. (I used to have to work at 7 A.M. at some of my engineering jobs!) However, it's pretty standard in the industry—kind of a hold-over from the old-school culture of "work all night and drag yourself into the office the next day by around noon." Depending on how energetic I feel, I will sometimes get to work earlier than 10 because the mornings are *the best* time to get uninterrupted work done—for example detailed system design or anything that requires me to have some silent alone time to solve.

I tend to spend the mornings trying to catch up on important things that might have been left hanging the afternoon before, or to get a jump on stuff that must get done today. Once people start arriving in the office, it's only a matter of time before I need to get out and about and check up on how tasks are going, see if people are having any problems, and otherwise attend to business of the day. Depending on the phase of the project, we may have "scrum" meetings first thing in the morning. These are quick stand-up meetings where we go around the room and people say what they are working on and whether they have any questions or problems. For example, a programmer or artist might be working on a game screen, but they just realized they need some information from the game designer(s) about what that screen needs to contain and how that screen will work.

Having daily meetings helps make sure that people are talking and don't waste time when they are stuck.

If everything is going well with the team, I usually check in before lunch with the creative director/studio head. He and I handle all the business development, which means writing game proposals and sending them out to publishers or "pitching" them. Pitching just means meeting with publishers and trying to get them excited about a game idea so they will hire us to make it. If there are pitches we are in the middle of writing, we'll brainstorm some ideas or discuss additions and changes that need to be made to the pitch document. Then I'll make notes to address them later in the day when I get some time. During our discussion, we also may discuss budget issues for the current project, such as whether a programmer needs a new computer, a designer needs a Wii test-kit, or an artist needs a CinTiq drawing surface.

Lunch usually sneaks up pretty fast since we start so late in the morning. Lunch is often a good time to relax with coworkers, talk about cool games or movies, or network with friends and colleagues from other companies to hear about how their projects are going.

During the afternoon, I usually have a chance to do some design and writing work while everyone cranks away on their tasks. Several times a day, I usually check in with the lead designer on the Wii game, and we'll discuss gameplay issues and talk about anything that needs to be resolved. Often we have spirited debates about whether a feature is good or bad, or how it can be improved, and so on. Lately, we've been working on things like how fast should the character's vehicle turn, what arrangement of screen items looks best (e.g., lap counter, boost meter, timer, mini-map), and also which levels/tracks seem to be fun and which ones still need some reworking or improvement. Because we work at a small company and close by each other, we tend to tackle things as they come up rather than scheduling meetings. That goes for the whole team—we try to use verbal communication and instant messages more so than email, and email more so than meetings. Meetings are held only when we need to get several different people together at the same time and have a clear outcome in mind—otherwise, meetings can waste a lot of people's time.

If I'm lucky, the game design issues of the day might involve control tuning, level review, or other hands-on things that are the real fun part about making video games. And I prefer those things to scheduling and management anytime—but keeping a team of people going in the right direction is hugely important, so I have to be careful to prioritize around the whole team and not just what I like to do the most.

Every single day I usually have some desk chats with programmers or artists. Being a game designer means you are constantly working directly with programmers and artists—you describe how a game feature will work, and they have to implement it. So you are constantly working details out, checking on progress, and answering questions. Coordinating with your team members is often 50 percent or more of your work, so I don't advise super shy or loner-types to be a game designer—it will be hard to be effective. Designing the feature is only half the battle in getting it made, and you constantly have to be the champion for your design, willing to explain its benefits, describe its intricate details, and also shift your direction at a moment's notice when a programmer points out your idea won't work (it happens to the best of us).

The workday here formally ends at 6 P.M., but I often will stay late to take care of pressing issues or get a little more quiet time at the end of the day. However, I've learned over time that working on video games is a marathon not a sprint—it's best to go home and get some rest so that you can come back to work the next day and be productive. Staying too late can make you a zombie the next day, and studies have shown that working high amounts of overtime eventually makes you less productive than if you just worked a normal day. Video game creation is a highly mental and creative occupation, so when your brain is on autopilot, it's really hard to get anything meaningful done, unlike a lot of other industries and jobs.

Q. What do you like least and most about work as a game designer?

A. Least: The game industry has a long history of burning people out by overworking them—making video games is not easy and often requires herculean efforts to finish things on time and in a way that makes a game everyone can be proud of. There are still people around who think if you aren't working 12-hour days seven days a week, then you could be doing more. You have to be careful not to put yourself so much into your job that you burn yourself out in five years and then have nothing left to give to game development. It's a real battle. Fortunately, quality of life issues are much more center stage these days, and many companies have come to realize that keeping good employees means treating them well. Still, sometimes you just have to pony up and move mountains to get a game shipped on time, and those periods can be physically, mentally, and emotionally draining.

Most: There are many things I absolutely love about working in games. It's hard to know where to begin, really. Working around talented and creative people is fantastic—it's a lot of fun to interact with artists, programmers, and other designers. So many of them are fascinating, intelligent, and bring a real energy to the office. It's fun to walk by a desk filled with crazy action figures, look at a painter working on his CinTiq, talk to a programmer about solving some crazily complex technical problem involving hexadecimal memory addresses, and then shift right into a debate about the merits of the latest game or movie. A creative workplace has a creative, energetic vibe, and it's wonderful. I've worked in very traditional, stoic offices before as an engineer, and I am much happier in a more dynamic work environment.

The day-to-day variety of work and problem solving is also purely awesome to me. I have an active mind, and I just love how each day brings new challenges, each game feature requires new decisions, and each hour might bring up a completely different issue that needs solved. Game development is such a combined art and science, and "fighting the good fight" to make a good game is something that takes 100 percent of my mental capacity and keeps me intrigued and energized (and sometimes maddeningly frustrated!). I also really like the blend of technical and creative tasks that a game designer has to do.

Finally, working on a game and seeing it get released, played, and (hopefully) appreciated by consumers is incredible.

Q. What are the most important personal and professional qualities for game designers?

A. Passion: You have to love games. To be a game designer, you need to be fascinated not only with playing them, but also in deconstructing how they work, what makes a successful mechanic or character or story, and so on. What are the new hot games doing? What did old classic games do well? And so on.

Talent: Enjoying playing games is not enough to become a successful game designer. There are millions and millions of people who love to play games. I hate to be blunt, but if you want to be successful in game development, you need to find an area of game development that you have a talent for—that could be design, programming, modeling, animation, writing, testing, producing, and so on. You may not know your talents yet—and I encourage you to try things out and find them—but you must develop a skill to become a valuable game developer. Enthusiasm is not enough by itself...but it can get you places by making you work hard to develop your talent(s)!

Perseverance: Breaking into the industry takes a mix of talent and luck and networking. It took me years to break in, and I have colleagues that got in on their first try. You just never know, so you have to keep slogging after what you want and not give up when an interview goes badly, or your resume doesn't get looked at by your favorite company, and so on. Don't give up! This perseverance will also serve you really well once you are in the industry, because making a good game takes a mix of talent and luck.

Communication: Unless you are a balancing guru or a strong analyst or other very rare type of designer, almost every day of your design career will involve coordinating with the other designers, artists, and programmers on your team. If you hate being part of a team, you really should concentrate on hobby or indie-development that allows you to do your own thing—for example, this is something I love about designing board games on the side . . . I can do whatever I want! But when you are working on a video game with anywhere from six to 166 people on your team, being a good teammate is a huge part of being a good game designer. You need to provide the programmers with what they need, talk nicely with the artists about how a piece of art works for or against your feature, and so on. A maverick, abrasive game designer will quickly find themselves without the respect of their teammates, and that makes day-to-day life incredibly difficult. That doesn't mean never fighting for what you want or even refusing to compromise—you just have to pick your battles and be willing to communicate.

Q. What have been some of the most interesting or rewarding things that have happened to you while working as a game designer?

A. When my first digital game, *Age of Empires: The Age of Kings DS,* was released, I went down to Best Buy and purchased a copy and took a picture at the cash register. It was a surreal experience for me because it was the culmination of literally years and years of work (trying to break into the industry and then creating the game). It was a super feeling and I took a moment to stand back and take some pride and satisfaction for reaching a personal goal.

Another great experience was accepting a "Game Design of the Year" award at the first Canadian Awards for the Electronic and Animated Arts ceremony hosted by William Shatner. I accepted the award with my then creative director, Trent Ward, and my fellow designer Eric Emery. Although the award itself wasn't even a blip in the industry, it was a black-tie party and a generally fun event, and it felt great to chum around with my coworkers and celebrate some hard work.

Directors

OVERVIEW

Directors are the overall managers of any animation project—whether it's a video game, a commercial, music video, or a film. They supervise the creative work or performance of artists, animators, designers, writers, voice actors, and members of the production or technical staff. Directors approve work done at all stages of production, or may give additional guidance if the work falls short of their vision for the project. They work closely with producers to meet project goals. Depending on the size and scope of a project, there may be more than one director assigned to manage a particular department or task.

HISTORY

In the early days of animation, animators handled most or all of the job duties of making a movie—including what are now considered the duties of directors, producers, sound workers, voice actors, and other workers. The legendary animator Walt Disney, for example, drew the artwork for his early Mickey Mouse animated shorts, voiced the characters and created sound effects, and supervised any other workers that were needed to prepare the animated shorts for release in movie theaters.

But by the time Walt Disney Company released *Snow White and the Seven Dwarfs* (1937), which many consider to be the first feature-length animated film, directorial positions were more clearly defined. It took hundreds of animation professionals to create this groundbreaking film, and directors and art directors were needed to manage staff, brainstorm and implement creative decisions, and

School Subjects
Art
English

Personal Skills
Artistic
Leadership/management

Work Environment
Primarily indoors
One location with some
travel

Minimum Education Level
Bachelor's degree

Salary Range
$30,250 to $85,000 to
$200,000+

Certification or Licensing
None available

Outlook
Faster than the average

DOT
143, 164

GOE
01.01.01, 01.05.01

NOC
5131

O*NET-SOC
27-1011.00, 27-2012.02

oversee a variety of other related tasks. Many early animation directors came from the ranks of animators. For example, David Dodd Hand, the supervising director of *Snow White,* started his career in the animation industry by animating the *Andy Gump* series, then worked at Walter Bray Studios (another pioneering animation studio), before heading to Walt Disney in 1930.

Today, the presence of an experienced director can be the difference between the success and failure of an animation project. Hollywood animation directors such as Andrew Stanton (*WALL-E, Finding Nemo, A Bug's Life)* and Brad Bird *(Ratatouille, The Incredibles, Iron Giant)* earn top salaries and industry acclaim for their work. Others find success in directing television shows, music videos, or commercials. Like Walt Disney in the old days, some directors still also serve as writers, producers, and voice actors to ensure that their creative vision is successfully brought to the screen.

The artistic elements of computer and video games have come a long way from *Pong* graphics, where a simple moving blip on the screen entertained early gamers. Today's games not only have to be challenging, engaging, and fun, but they must be visually interesting, realistic, and flashy. While some games still incorporate "cute" characters in the vein of *Q*bert* or *Pac-Man,* the majority of game characters are now human. Figures are pictured with bulging muscles, realistic wounds, or, in the case of many *Final Fantasy* characters, have sex appeal. This realism is the work of huge teams of talented artists that all work together on the completion of a single game. As these teams grew, someone was needed to direct the efforts of these workers and ensure the process, quality, and productivity of the department. Thus, the career of art director developed to oversee this important aspect of game creation.

THE JOB

There are many types of directors employed in animation-related industries. The following paragraphs detail specialties in the computer and video game, advertising, and film and television industries. It is important to remember that some jobs are industry specific, while others may be found in more than one animation-related industry.

Computer and Video Game Industry

Art directors are responsible for making sure all visual aspects of a computer or video game meet the expectations of the producers, and ultimately, the client. The art director works directly and indirectly with all artists on a project, such as 2D and 3D artists, model makers,

Animation Film Festivals

Animation Block Party
http://www.animationblock.com

The Animation Show
http://www.animationshow.com

Annecy International Animated Film Festival
http://www.annecy.org

Asian Animation Film Festival
http://www.colum.edu/asianartsandmedia/Asian_Animation_
  Film_Festival.php

Film Festival World: Animation
http://www.filmfestivalworld.com/animation

International Animation Festival Hiroshima
http://hiroanim.org/en

Melbourne International Animation Festival
http://www.miaf.net

Ottawa International Animation Festival
http://ottawa.awn.com

Platform International Animation Festival
http://platformfestival.com/home.aspx

Red Stick Animation Festival
http://redstickfestival.org

Seoul International Cartoon and Animation Festival
http://www.sicaf.or.kr/2009/eng

South Beach International Animation Film Festival
http://www.southbeachanimationfest.com

Spike and Mike's Sick and Twisted Festival of Animation
http://www.spikeandmike.com

Stuttgart Festival of Animated Film
http://www.itfs.de/en

Tecnotoon Animation Fest
http://www.tecnotoon.com/animation_fest.htm

Waterloo Festival for Animated Cinema
http://www.wfac.ca

West Virginia Flash Animation Festival
http://www.westliberty.edu/wvfestival

texture artists, and character animators. They supervise both in-house and off-site staff, handle management issues, and oversee the entire artistic production process. Depending on the size of the company, the director may work as a staff artist in addition to handling managerial tasks. But generally, the director's main responsibilities focus on board meetings rather than on the drawing board.

Art directors must be skilled in and knowledgeable about design, illustration, computers, research, and writing in order to supervise the work of their department. They need to be skilled in classic art forms, such as illustration and sculpture, while still familiar with computer art tools.

To coordinate all artistic contributions of a computer or video game, art directors may begin with the client's concept or develop one in collaboration with the executive producer. Once the concept is established, the next step is to decide on the most effective way to create it. If the project is to create a sequel to a preexisting game, past animations and illustrations must be taken into consideration and reevaluated for use in the new game.

After deciding what needs to be created, art directors must hire talented staff that can accomplish these tasks. Because the visual aspects of a game are so important, the art department can be quite large, even just for the creation of a single game.

The process of creating a computer or video game begins in much the same way that a television show or film is created. The art director may start with the client's concept or create one in-house in collaboration with staff members. Once a concept has been created, the art director sketches a rough storyboard based on the producer's ideas, and the plan is presented for review to the creative director. The next step is to develop a finished storyboard, with larger and more detailed frames (the individual scenes) in color. This storyboard is presented to the client for review and used as a guide for the executive producer.

Managing a team of animators and other artists, *creative directors* give great input in the style, design, and gaming experience of computer and video games. Creative directors make certain that games follow an approved style or specification, such as a reoccurring character, theme, or function. They work with the art director to define the desired animation style of the project; and the producers to set goals within the given budget and schedule.

Animated Films, Television Shows, Commercials, and Music Videos

Casting directors audition actors and actresses for animated productions. They recommend actors to producers and directors. But unlike traditional film and television casting directors, these professionals typically focus on an actor's voice and audio expressiveness, not their looks or physical acting abilities. Casting directors find just the right actor to voice a character in an animated film or video game. For example, they might seek an actor with an offbeat, even squeaky, voice for the role of a wacky alien or one with a deep, commanding voice for the role of a military leader or teacher. They also seek actors who can express emotion—happiness, anger, excitement, sadness, etc.—via their voices. Some films now combine live action with animation; in these instances, a casting director will search for an actor with a combination of the right look, voice, and acting ability.

Production designers are responsible for all visual aspects of on-screen productions. Working with directors, producers, and other professionals, production designers interpret scripts and create or select settings in order to visually convey the story or the message. *Art directors* are the top assistants of production designers; they ensure that the production designer's vision is implemented.

Cel animation is the traditional form of animation that dominated the animation industry until the 1990s when it was replaced by computer-generated animation technology. It is estimated that 95 percent of major animated features today are created using computer-generated animation technology, but this does not mean that cel animation is extinct. Cel-animated features such as *Lilo & Stitch* (2002) have proven that there is still a niche market for this animation technique. *Directors of cel animation* have great control of cel animation projects, specifically during the production of storyboards and animation sequences. They work with writers from the story department on ideas and the development of a story line. They also supervise artistic elements of a project, such as approving all character sketches and background painting. Directors of cel animation may delegate work assignments to members of the animation and layout staff and make sure all work is completed on schedule. They also work closely with the project's producers on staffing and other issues.

Directors of computer-generated animation manage animators and artists on a daily basis, checking that their work meets design and thematic standards. They also work with production designers, art directors, and other production staff to make sure the project is manageable and meeting scheduling demands. Directors of computer-generated animation are knowledgeable about different software programs such as 3D Package and Maya.

Even after an animated work is completed, there is still much to be done before feature films, commercials, videos, or television shows are considered "done." The *director of postproduction* supervises the processing and delivery of dailies to the proper departments, coordinates and implements editing schedules, and monitors the cost of all postproduction work to stay within budget.

REQUIREMENTS

High School

Directors' careers are rather nontraditional. There is no standard training path, no normal progression up an industry ladder leading to the director's job. At the very least, a high school diploma, while not tech-

Andrew Stanton, the director of *Wall-E*, poses for photographers at the animated film's premiere. *(Sipa, AP Images)*

nically required if you wish to become a director, will still probably be indispensable to you in terms of the background and education it signifies. As is true of all artists, especially those in mediums as popular as the computer and video game industry or the television and film industries, you will need to have rich and varied experience in order to create works that are intelligently crafted, entertaining, and speak to people of many different backgrounds and ages. In high school, courses in English, art, theater, and history will give you a good foundation. Furthermore, a high school diploma will be necessary if you decide to go on to film school or pursue a degree in video game design.

Postsecondary Training

You do not need a college degree to work as a director in the computer and video game industry, but with competition increasing for employment in this popular field, it is a good idea to earn a degree—or at least take a few classes—in game design, programming, or related subjects. In addition to course work at the college level, many universities and professional art schools offer graduates or students in their final year a variety of workshop projects or internships. These opportunities provide students with the chance to work on real games, develop their personal styles, and add to their work experience. Animation World Network offers a database of animation schools at its Web site (http://schools.awn.com). Another good source of schools can be found at the International Game Developers Association's Web site (http://archives.igda.org/breakingi n/resource_schools.php).

Film, television, music video, and commercial directors do not need a college degree to enter the field. Some of today's top directors are self-taught or have learned their skills on the job. But since this field is very competitive, it is a good idea to earn a degree or at least take some college classes that will teach you about directing. Film studies and animation programs are offered at universities and art institutes across the country. Traditional film schools may also offer specialized programs for aspiring animation directors.

Other Requirements

The work of a director requires creativity, imagination, curiosity, and a sense of adventure. Directors must be able to work with all sorts of specialized equipment and computer software as well as communicate their ideas to other directors, producers, designers, and studio or company executives.

The ability to work well with different types of people and situations is a must for directors. They must always be up to date on new techniques, technologies, and trends. Because deadlines are a constant part of the work, an ability to handle stress and pressure well is key.

The visual aspects of a computer or video game or animated film can be the very things that make it sell. For this reason, accuracy and attention to detail are important parts of the director's job. When the visuals are innovative and clean, the public either clamors for it or pays no notice. But when a project's visuals are done poorly or sloppily, people will notice, even if they have had no artistic training, and the game will not sell or the film will not be watched.

EXPLORING

If you are a would-be director, the most obvious opportunity for exploration lies in your own imagination. Being drawn to animated films or video games and captivated by the process of how they are made is the beginning of a director's journey.

In high school and beyond, carefully study and pay attention to animated films and video games. Watch as many animated films and shows on television, in theaters, and on the Internet as possible. Play different types of computer and video games. Try to determine why certain games make you want to keep playing, while others make you want to move on and try a different game. Do the same with animated features and shorts. Rent animated classics and surf the Internet to watch animated shorts and feature-length films.

You can also read general trade publications about the film and television industry such as *Variety* (http://www.variety.com) and *Hollywood Reporter* (http://www.hollywoodreporter.com) or specialized publications about animation and/or game design such as *Animation Journal* (http://www.animationjournal.com), *Animation World* (http://mag.awn.com), *Game Developer* (http://www.gdmag.com), GameZone Online (http://www.gamezone.com), *Computer Graphics World* (http://www.cgw.com), and *GameInformer* (http://www.gameinformer.com). The Directors Guild of America's official publication *DGA Magazine* (http://www.dga.org) contains useful information for directors in the film and television industries.

Another way to explore is by researching the career on the Internet. Visit the Web site of the International Game Developers Association (http://archives.igda.org/breakingin) to check out "Breaking In: Preparing for Your Career in Games." This free online publication can give you an overview of the different jobs available in the visual arts and features job profiles and interviews of workers in the field.

During summers, many colleges and universities offer camps and workshops for high school students interested in computer and video game design and animation. Contact schools near you to see what programs are available.

EMPLOYERS

Directors working in the computer and video game industry work all over the country for companies large and small. Major entertainment software publishers include Electronic Arts, Nintendo of America, Atari, Sony, Activision Blizzard, THQ, Take-Two Interactive Software Inc., Microsoft, and Konami Digital Entertainment-America. Jobs should be available at these companies as well as with online services and interactive networks, which are growing rapidly.

Employment as a director in the film and television industries is usually on a freelance or contractual basis. Directors find work, for example, with animation studios (both major and independent), at television stations and cable networks (such as Nickelodeon and the Cartoon Network), through advertising agencies, with record companies (music videos), and through the creation of their own independent animation projects.

STARTING OUT

Since a director's job requires a great deal of experience, it is usually not considered an entry-level position. Typically, a person on a career track toward director is hired as an assistant to an established director. Recent graduates wishing to enter the game or animated film or television industries should develop what is called a demo reel. This is a type of portfolio, only the work is interactive and shows moving

Books to Read

Beck, Jerry. *Animation Art: From Pencil to Pixel, the World of Cartoon, Anime, and CGI.* New York: Collins Design, 2004.

Furniss, Maureen. *The Animation Bible: A Practical Guide to the Art of Animating from Flipbooks to Flash.* New York: Harry N. Abrams, 2008.

Laramee, Francois Dominic. *Secrets of the Game Business.* 2d ed. Florence, Ky.: Charles River Media, 2005.

Levy, David. *Animation Development: From Pitch to Production.* New York: Allworth Press, 2009.

Levy, David. *Your Career in Animation: How to Survive and Thrive.* New York: Allworth Press, 2006.

Rush, Alice, David Hodgson, and Bryan Stratton. *Paid to Play: An Insider's Guide to Video Game Careers.* Roseville, Calif.: Prima Games, 2006.

Sacks, Terence J. *Opportunities in Cartooning & Animation Careers.* New York: McGraw-Hill, 2007.

animations and backgrounds as opposed to pictures of static images. Demo reels can show your skill in composition, color, light, motion, presentation, and craftsmanship. It should reflect a wide breadth of styles and show work in more than just one genre of game or animation style. This will show that you are versatile as well as creative.

Remember that directors have done their time in lower positions before advancing to the level of director, so be willing to do your time and acquire credentials by working on various projects. Starting out as an intern or assistant is a good way to get experience and develop skills.

ADVANCEMENT

Again, directors are not entry-level workers. They usually have years of experience working at lower-level jobs in the field before gaining the knowledge needed to supervise projects. This experience will help them manage their artistic staff and solve problems quickly when necessary.

While some may be content upon reaching the position of director, many directors take on even more responsibility within their organizations, become producers or studio executives, develop original multimedia programs, or create their own games or animated features.

Many people who get to the position of director do not advance beyond the title but move on to work at larger game developers or on more prestigious projects. Competition for positions at companies that have strong reputations continues to be keen because of the sheer number of talented people interested in the field. At smaller game developers or animation studios, the competition may be less intense, since candidates are competing primarily against others in the local market.

In the motion picture industry, advancement often comes with recognition. Directors who work on well-received movies are given awards as well as further job offers. The most well-known trophy is the Academy Award: the Oscar. Oscars are awarded in a variety of categories, including one for best animated film, and are given annually at a gala to recognize the outstanding accomplishments of those in the field. The International Animated Film Society, ASIFA-Hollywood also offers awards, called Annies, for the best animated film of the year.

EARNINGS

The International Game Developers Association (IGDA) reports that art directors with six or more years of experience can earn $68,000 or more. Creative directors with six or more years' experience can earn up to $80,000. Skilled directors with many years of experience working with some of the larger game developers can earn salaries of $200,000 or more.

Earnings for film, television, music video, and advertising/commercial directors vary greatly. Most Hollywood film directors are members of the Directors Guild of America (DGA), and salaries (as well as hours of work and other employment conditions) are usually negotiated by this union. Generally, contracts provide for minimum weekly salaries. The minimum weekly salary for directors was $4,726 in 2009. This figure increases based on the cost of the picture being made. Keep in mind that because directors are freelancers, they may have no income for many weeks out of the year. Although contracts usually provide only for the minimum rate of pay, most directors earn more, and they often negotiate extra conditions. Directors working under DGA contracts also receive paid vacation days, lodging and meals while filming, and access to pension and health insurance plans.

The U.S. Department of Labor (DoL) reports that the median annual salary of film directors and producers was $64,430 in 2008. Among this group, the lowest paid 10 percent earned less than $30,250, and the highest paid 25 percent earned more than $105,070. The DoL reports the following mean annual salaries for directors by industry: advertising, $107,520; motion picture and video industries, $98,930; cable and other subscription programming, $84,420; and television broadcasting, $71,860.

The DoL reports that art directors in the motion picture and video industries earned mean annual salaries of $101,780 in 2008, and those employed in the advertising industry earned $92,500.

Benefits for salaried directors include vacation and sick time, health, and sometimes dental, insurance, and pension or 401(k) plans. Self-employed directors must provide their own benefits. Freelance directors who are union members often receive benefits such as health insurance as part of their union agreements

WORK ENVIRONMENT

Directors who are employed in animation-related industries usually work in studios or offices. Their work areas are typically comfortable and well lit and ventilated.

The work of the director is considered glamorous and prestigious, and directors—especially in the film and television industries—have been known to become quite famous. But directors work under great stress, meeting deadlines, staying within budgets, and resolving problems among staff. "Nine-to-five" definitely does not describe a day in the life of a director; 16-hour days (and more) are not uncommon. Because directors are ultimately responsible for so much, schedules often dictate that they become immersed in their work around the clock, from preproduction to final cut. Nonetheless, those able to make it in the industry find their work to be extremely enjoyable and satisfying.

OUTLOOK

Computer and video game companies will always need talented directors to help create games. Directors with both creative and technical skills will have the best employment prospects.

Employment of directors in the motion picture and video industries is expected to increase faster than the average for all careers through 2016, according to the U.S. Department of Labor. More directors will be needed because the number of animated films, television shows, and commercials that are being produced is increasing. Employment for directors in the advertising industry is expected to grow about as fast as the average through 2016.

FOR MORE INFORMATION

Visit the guild's Web site to learn more about the industry and DGA-sponsored training programs and to read selected articles from DGA Quarterly.

Directors Guild of America (DGA)
7920 Sunset Boulevard
Los Angeles, CA 90046-3300
Tel: 310-289-2000
http://www.dga.org

For industry information, contact
Entertainment Software Association
575 Seventh Street, NW, Suite 300
Washington, DC 20004-1611
Email: esa@theesa.com
http://www.theesa.com

For information on the Annie Awards, contact
International Animated Film Society-ASIFA Hollywood
2114 West Burbank Boulevard
Burbank, CA 91506-1232
Tel: 818-842-8330

Email: info@asifa-hollywood.org
http://www.asifa-hollywood.org

For career advice and industry information, contact
International Game Developers Association
19 Mantua Road
Mt. Royal, NJ 08061-1006
Tel: 856-423-2990
http://www.igda.org

This union represents scenic artists, scenic and production designers, art directors, costume designers, lighting designers, sound designers, projection designers, computer artists, industrial workers, and art department coordinators working in film, television, industrial shows, theatre, opera, ballet, commercials, and exhibitions.
United Scenic Artists Local 829
29 West 38th Street, 15th Floor
New York, NY 10018-5504
Tel: 212-581-0300
http://www.usa829.org

Editors

OVERVIEW

There are two main types of *editors* working in animation-related industries: those who edit computer and video games and animated films, television shows, commercials, and music videos (referred to as *animation editors* in this article) and those who edit animation-related articles, reviews, books, game manuals, technical documentation, and Web documents (referred to as *text editors* in this article). Some editors may be full-time, salaried workers, but many are employed on a freelance basis.

HISTORY

Early animated film editing was done by directors, studio technicians, animators, or other animation professionals. Now every animated film has a specialized editor who is responsible for the continuity and clarity of the film. Animated shorts also require editing, but this editing is often done by the film's creator, who also often serves as its writer, director, producer, marketer, etc.

Text editors have been needed in animation-related industries ever since the first magazines and books were published, marketing materials and game manuals were written, and computer and video games and animated films were released. Today, they play a key role in the success of print and online publications.

THE JOB

Animation editors who are employed in the film, television, advertising, music, or related industries work closely with producers and directors throughout an entire project. These editors assist in the earliest phase, called preproduction, and during the production phase, when actual filming/animation occurs. Their skills are in the greatest demand during postproduction, the completion of primary filming/animation. During preproduction, editors meet with producers to learn about the objectives of the animated film, short, music video, or commercial. If the project is a feature-length animated film, such as *Ice Age,* the editor must understand the story line. The producer may explain the larger scope of the project so that the editor knows the best way to approach the work when it is time to edit the film. In consultation with the director, editors may discuss the best way to present the screenplay or script. They may discuss different settings, scenes, or camera angles (in traditional animation) even before work on the project begins. With this kind of preparation, animation editors are ready to practice their craft as soon as the production phase is complete. Feature-length animated films, of course, take much more time to edit than television commercials or music videos. Therefore, some editors may spend months on one project, while others may work on several shorter projects simultaneously.

Game animation editors are responsible for editing computer and video games using the AVID software or other editing software. Once animated characters and backgrounds are designed, the action sequences animated according to the storyboard and script, and all voice-over work completed, the project is given over to the capable hands of editors. During this postproduction phase, editors are responsible for taking animated clips, and putting them into proper sequence. Often operating under tight deadlines, editors have the delicate task of working with a designer's vision of the project. It's an important balancing act, since oftentimes the success of a video game is due to skillful editing. Since editing work in the game industry is so closely linked to the design and technical layout of a game, editing may be handled by a game's designer, with assistance from programmers and other workers. Game animation editors may also help create commercials or trailers that advertise games on television or the Internet. These are typically 30 or 60 seconds in length, which requires the editor to communicate the content and feel of a game in a succinct, yet entertaining, manner.

Text editors who work in animation-related industries can be divided into two major areas: those who are employed by the media to edit articles, feature stories, reviews, or books about products, trends, and other topics and those who are employed by animation companies, game companies and developers, and related employers to edit user manuals, marketing materials, and other documents.

Text editors who work for print and online publications ensure that text provided by writers is suitable in content, format, and style for the intended audiences—whether they are employed by a magazine geared toward teen gamers or publications for animation insiders. They might have specialized titles—such as *game review editor, hardware editor, platform/console editor, or news editor*—based on the types of writing they edit. Some editors are full-time, salaried employees of publishers, while many others may work on a freelance basis. As freelancers, editors run their own businesses and need business skills to keep track of their financial accounts and market their work.

Text editors who work for animation companies, film and television studios, advertising agencies, game companies and developers, and educational software publishers edit a variety of materials. An editor for a company such as Warner Bros. Animation Studios might edit in-house technical documents, user manuals, technical documents, Web site content, marketing materials, game or DVD packaging, and other documents. *Technical editors* are text editors who take raw information about a subject, and edit this data to create software manuals, procedure manuals, help systems and tutorials online, as well as trade books and documents. Technical editors do most of the writing, though they may consult with training developers, graphics personnel, or programmers for some of the content. Others may edit consumer publications published by game companies such as Nintendo or Sega.

REQUIREMENTS
High School
Because animation editing requires creativity along with technical skills, you should take English, speech, theater, and other courses that will allow you to develop writing skills. Art and photography classes will involve you with visual media. Because of the technical nature of animation editing, take computer classes to become comfortable and confident using basic animation editing programs.

If you are interested in becoming a text editor, take general science, social studies, computer science, literature, foreign languages, and typing classes while in high school. Editors must be expert communicators, so you should excel in English if you wish to work in this career. You must learn to write extremely well, since you will be correcting and even rewriting the work of others. If they are offered at your school, take elective classes in writing or editing, such as creative writing, editing, journalism, and business communications.

Postsecondary Training

Some studios and game companies require those seeking positions as animation editors to have a bachelor's degree although many believe that on-the-job experience and contacts in the industry are the best guarantees of securing lasting employment. Two- and four-year colleges often offer courses or majors in film or animation editing.

Most text editing jobs require a college education. Many employers prefer that you have a broad liberal arts background or majors in English, literature, history, philosophy, or one of the social sciences. Other employers desire communications or journalism training in college. Technical editors may have degrees in computer science, animation, game design, computer programming, or related fields. If you are interested in a career as an editor in an animation-related industry, you should take courses on animation and game design in college. In addition to formal course work, most employers look for practical editing experience. If you have worked as an editor on high school or college newspapers, yearbooks, or literary magazines, you will make a better candidate, as well as if you have worked for small community newspapers, even in an unpaid position. Many game companies, animation studios, book publishers, magazines, and newspapers have summer internship programs that provide valuable training if you want to learn about the field. Interns do many simple tasks, such as running errands and answering phones, but some may be asked to perform research, conduct interviews, or even write or edit some minor pieces.

Other Requirements

Animation editors should be able to work cooperatively with other creative people when editing a film or video game. They should remain open to suggestions and guidance, while also maintaining their confidence in the presence of other professionals. A successful editor has an understanding of the history of animation (or the video game industry if they want to enter this field) and a feel for the narrative form in general. Computer animation skills are also important, as well as a desire to keep up with the latest technology and editing techniques in the field.

You must be detail oriented to succeed as a text editor. You must also be patient, since you may have to spend hours synthesizing information into the written word or turning a few pages of near-gibberish or technical jargon into powerful, elegant English. If you are the kind of person who can't sit still, you probably will not succeed in this career. To be a good editor, you must be a self-starter who is not afraid to make decisions. You must be good not only at identifying problems but also at solving them, so you must be creative.

Depending on the employer, union membership may be required to work as an animation or text editor.

EXPLORING

Many high schools have film or animation clubs, and some have cable television stations affiliated with the school district. Often school-run television channels give students the opportunity to create and edit short programs. Check out what's available at your school. One of the best ways to prepare for a career as an animation editor is to read widely. By reading literature, you will get a sense of the different ways in which stories can be presented. Some high schools even offer film, game design, or animation classes. You should also become very familiar with popular animated films and games. Don't just watch these films or play these games; rather, study them, paying close attention to the decisions the editors made in piecing together the scenes or action. Large animation studios and game companies occasionally offer positions for volunteers or student interns. Most people in the animation industry start out doing minor tasks helping with production. These production assistants get the opportunity to observe a variety of animation professionals at work. By working closely with an animation editor, a production assistant can learn about the overall operations of an animation studio or game company as well as specific animation editing techniques.

Another way to learn more about editing careers and animation-related industries is to read publications about the field. There are many online magazines that cover these fields. Some popular publications include *Game Developer* (http://www.gdmag.com), *Animation World* (http://mag.awn.com), GameZone Online (http://www.gamezone.com), *Computer Graphics World* (http://www.cgw.com), *GameInformer* (http://www.gameinformer.com), *VideoGameNews* (http://videogamenews.com), *CARTOON* (http://www.asifa-hollywood.org), *Animation Magazine* (http://www.animationmagazine.net), and *CinemaEditor* (http://www.ace-filmeditors.org/newace/mag_Main.html). You also might want to read the online resource "Breaking In: Preparing For Your Career in Games," which is available at the International Game Developers Association's Web site (http://archives.igda.org/breakingin).

You can explore the career of text editor by working as an editor for school newspapers, yearbooks, and literary magazines. Perhaps you can even land a volunteer or part-time job editing for a local newspaper or community newsletter. You can also start a blog or Web site about animation or gaming, ask your friends to contribute, and get practice as an editor by editing their work.

EMPLOYERS

Animation editors work for game companies, animation studios, television networks, advertising agencies, and related employers. Many animation editors who have worked for a studio or post-production company for several years often become independent contractors. They offer their services on a per-job basis to producers of films, television shows, and advertisements, negotiating their own fees, and typically have purchased or leased their own editing equipment. Animation editors may develop ongoing working relationships with directors or producers who hire them from one project to another.

Text editors are employed by entertainment software publishers, animation companies, computer and video companies, book and magazine publishers, newspapers, online publications, and any other organization that requires the skills of an editor.

STARTING OUT

With a minimum of a high school diploma or a degree from a two-year college, you can apply for entry-level jobs at many film, television, or game studios. Most studios, however, will not consider people for animation editor positions without a bachelor's degree or several years of on-the-job experience. Larger studios may offer apprenticeships for animation editors. Apprentices have the opportunity to see the work of the animation editor up close. The animator editor may eventually assign some of his or her minor duties to the apprentice, while the editor makes the larger decisions. After a few years, the apprentice may be promoted to animation editor or may apply for a position as an editor at other studios. Those who have completed bachelor's or master's degrees have typically gained hands-on experience through school projects. Another benefit of going to school is that contacts that you make while in school, both through your school's career services office and alumni, can be a valuable resource when you look for your first job. Your school's career services office may also have listings of job openings. Some studio work is union regulated. Therefore you may also want to contact union locals to find out about job requirements and openings.

Text editors should contact their college career services office or journalism or communications department for help with their job search. In addition, contacts that you make during an internship or summer job may provide employment leads. Aspiring text editors can also find job leads by visiting Web sites that offer job listings. These include GameJobs (http://www.gamejobs.com) and Gamasutra (http://www.gamasutra.com). Many people interested in employment in the game industry also attend the annual Game Developers Conference (http://www.gdconf.com) to network and learn more about internship and job opportunities.

ADVANCEMENT

Once animation editors have secured employment in their field, their advancement comes with further experience and greater recognition. Some animation editors develop good working relationships with directors or producers. These editors may be willing to leave the security of a studio job for the possibility of working one-on-one with the director or producer on a project. These opportunities often provide animation editors with the autonomy they may not get in their regular jobs. Some are willing to take a pay cut to work on a project they feel is important. Some editors choose to stay at their studios and advance through seniority to editing positions with higher salaries. They may be able to negotiate better benefits packages or to choose which projects they will work on. They may also choose which directors or game designers they wish to work with. In larger studios, they may train and supervise staffs of less experienced or apprentice editors.

Most text editors break into the field by working as editorial or production assistants. Editors usually have a better chance to advance at smaller companies or publications. Why? Because editors at these employers are typically assigned a variety of duties and, as a result, learn many skills. A typical advancement path for editors might include the following steps: editorial/production assistant, copy editor, senior copy editor, project editor, first assistant editor, managing editor, and editor in chief. Technical editors advance by working on longer and more complicated documents and by assuming managerial duties. Freelance or self-employed editors earn advancement in the form of larger fees or work on more prestigious publications as they gain exposure and establish their reputations.

EARNINGS

According to the U.S. Department of Labor, the median annual wage for animation editors employed in the film and television industries was $50,560 in 2008. A small percentage of editors earned less than $24,640 a year, while some earned more than $112,410. The most experienced and sought-after animation editors can command much higher salaries.

The U.S. Department of Labor reports that the median annual earnings for text editors employed in all industries were $49,990 in 2008. Salaries ranged from $28,090 or less to more than $95,490. Those who were employed by newspaper, periodical, book, and directory publishers had mean annual earnings of $57,150 in 2008.

Typical benefits for all types full-time, salaried editors include sick leave, vacation pay, and health, life, and disability insurance. Retirement plans may also be available, and some companies may match employees' contributions. Some companies may also offer stock-option plans. Freelance editors are responsible for providing their own medical, disability, and life insurance. They must also fund their own retirement plans.

WORK ENVIRONMENT

Animation editors do most of their work in studios at film, game, or postproduction companies using editing equipment. Studios are often small and cramped. Working hours vary widely, depending on the project. When working on an animated television series, for instance, editors may be required to work overtime, at night, or on weekends to finish the project by an assigned date. Many animated features are kept on tight production schedules that allow for steady work unless production falls behind.

Working conditions vary for text editors. They usually work a standard 40-hour week, but may have to log extensive overtime in order to meet production deadlines. Most editors work in well-lit, comfortable offices. Some have access to the latest computer technology, while others must use older equipment that may cause frustration at times.

OUTLOOK

Employment of animation editors in the motion picture and video industries is expected to increase about as fast as the average for all careers through 2016, according to the U.S. Department of Labor. More animated films, television shows, and commercials are being produced, which will create a need for qualified editors. Opportunities should also be good in the gaming industry, although some designers and directors handle editing responsibilities for games, which may reduce employment opportunities for editors at some companies.

Text editors play a very important role in animation-related industries. They help create coherent, error-free articles, books, advertising copy, game manuals, Web sites, and any other material that is written about the field. The U.S. Department of Labor predicts that employment for editors employed in all industries will experience little or no change compared to all occupations through 2016.

FOR MORE INFORMATION

ACE offers career and education information at its Web site, along with information about internship opportunities for college graduates, competitions, and sample articles from CinemaEditor *magazine.*

American Cinema Editors (ACE)
100 Universal City Plaza
Verna Fields Building 2282, Room 190
Universal City, CA 91608-1002
Tel: 818-777-2900
http://www.ace-filmeditors.org

For industry information, contact the following associations:
Entertainment Software Association
575 Seventh Street, NW, Suite 300
Washington, DC 20004-1611
Email: esa@theesa.com
http://www.theesa.com

Software & Information Industry Association
1090 Vermont Avenue, NW, 6th Floor
Washington, DC 20005-4095
Tel: 202-289-7442
http://www.siia.net

Visit the following Web site for comprehensive information on journalism careers, summer programs, and college journalism programs:
High School Journalism
http://www.highschooljournalism.org

For information on careers in the computer and game development industry, contact
International Game Developers Association
19 Mantua Road
Mt. Royal, NJ 08061-1006
Tel: 856-423-2990
http://www.igda.org

For additional information regarding online writing and journal-ism, check out the following Web site:

Online News Association
http://journalists.org/?

For information on awards and internships, contact
Society of Professional Journalists
Eugene S. Pulliam National Journalism Center
3909 North Meridian Street
Indianapolis, IN 46208-4011
Tel: 317-927-8000
http://www.spj.org

Graphics Programmers

OVERVIEW

Graphics programmers design software that allows computers to generate graphic designs, animations, charts, and illustrations for manufacturing, communications, entertainment, and engineering. They also develop computer applications that graphic designers use to create multimedia presentations, posters, logos, layouts for publication, and many other objects. Graphics programmers in the computer and video game industry focus on designing software and writing code in order to create the exciting action and elaborate settings of computer and video games.

HISTORY

Computers have been used to process large amounts of data in business, government, and education since the 1950s. It was only a matter of time before someone figured out a way to have fun with them. The computer and video game industry began to develop in the 1960s and 1970s, when computer programmers at some large universities, big companies, and government labs began designing games on mainframe computers. *Spacewar*, generally considered to be the first video game, was developed in 1962 by a team led by Steve Russell at Massachusetts Institute of Technology. Graphics of space ships flew through a starry sky on the video screen, the object of the game being to shoot down enemy ships. *Spacewar* quickly spread to other university computer labs and was very popular.

Computer and video games stepped out of the university setting and into the public realm in the early 1970s. In 1972 Nolan Bushnell founded the Atari company and created *Pong*, the first popular video arcade game. *Pong* required players to paddle electronic ping-pong balls back and forth across the video screen. The graphics were crude by today's standards, but the game was a big hit all over the country. In the years following, more games were developed, and most were designed for video arcade machines. It wasn't until the mid- to late 1970s that games for specially equipped TVs and personal computers (PCs) begin appearing. The Atari 2600, Intellivision, and the Commodore 64 were some of the early platforms used to play games at home. Games and their platforms continued to evolve, and the graphics improved as computer technology advanced. In the 1980s and 1990s game players were introduced to new systems and games from Nintendo, Sega, and Sony, as well as from some of the original computer and video game companies. Games were also developed for PCs at an increasing rate as PC sales increased. In 2001 computer software giant Microsoft released its Xbox platform and games. Computer game programmers were kept busy as they constantly strived to develop new ideas and come up with the next big computer and video game before another company did. This competition transformed the computer and video game industry: across all platforms, the rudimentary graphics and simple, action-driven premises of the early games had been replaced with cutting-edge animation, graphics, sound, and game strategy.

THE JOB

Graphics or graphics game programmers write the software necessary to implement the graphics in a computer or video game. The graphics programmer's job is similar to that of other computer programmers: determining what the computer will be expected to do and writing instructions for the computer that will allow it to carry out these functions. For a computer to perform any operation at all, detailed instructions must be written into its memory in a computer language, such as BASIC, COBOL, PASCAL, C++, HTML, Smalltalk, Java, or Assembly. The programmer is responsible for telling the computer exactly what to do. However, graphics are challenging—the programmer needs to project the appearance of three-dimensional objects inside of a two-dimensional display. They also need to accomplish this goal with writing code that allows for the highest quality of graphics but within the limitations of what can be displayed in real time on a computer.

In order to create graphics for a computer and video game, typically an artist or game designer will present the concept of what they are trying to achieve to the graphics programmer and expect that they will write the necessary code to accomplish the goal. Before actually writing code for part of a game, the programmer must analyze the artist/designer's request and the desired results. The graphics programmer must decide on how to approach it and plan what the computer will have to do to produce the desired results. They must pay attention to minute details and instruct the computer in each step of the process. These instructions are coded in one of several programming languages or implemented through the use of an Application Programming Interface (API), such as Direct 3D (which is the basis of the API on the Xbox and Xbox 360 console systems). When the graphics code is completed, the programmer tests its working practicality. If the graphics perform according to expectations and the artists and/or designers are satisfied with the end result, it is finished. If the graphics do not perform as anticipated, the graphics code will have to be debugged—that is, examined for errors that must be eliminated. Games that are designed to play on a platform other than a personal computer, such as a video game console, mobile communication device, arcade machine, or handheld gaming device, are then tested by the hardware manufacturer to ensure that all aspects of the game, including the graphics, perform well on the intended platform.

REQUIREMENTS

High School
If you are interested in graphics programming in the computer and video game industry, take classes that satisfy the admission requirements of the college or university that you plan to attend. Most major universities have requirements for English, mathematics, science, and foreign languages. Other classes that are useful include physics, statistics, logic, computer science, and, if available, drafting. Since graphics programmers have to have an artistic sense of layout and design, art and photography courses can also be helpful.

Postsecondary Training
A bachelor's degree in computer science or a related field is highly recommended for anyone wishing to enter the field of graphics programming. In fact, as programming for computer and video games becomes more complex, some employers prefer employees with graduate degrees. The U.S. Department of Labor reports that more

Top Employment Sectors for Animation Professionals

1. Computer and video game industry

2. Feature film character animation

3. Advertising/commercials

4. Television shows

Source: AnimationMentor.com

than 68 percent of computer programmers held a bachelor's degree or higher in 2006. It is not a good idea, however, to major in graphics programming exclusively, unless you plan to go on to earn a master's degree or doctorate in the field. According to the Special Interest Group on Computer Graphics, a division of the Association for Computing Machinery (ACM SIGGRAPH), it is better for you to concentrate on the area in which you plan to use computer graphics skills, such as art or engineering, rather than focusing on graphics classes.

Because there are many specialties within the field of computer graphics, such as mapmaking, animation, and computer-aided design, you should examine the courses of study offered in several schools before choosing the one you wish to attend. As more and more schools tailor programs specifically to the computer and video game industry, students now have the opportunity to earn a degree or certificate in this field. Graduate degrees with an emphasis in areas such as 3D graphics programming are very relevant to the rapidly evolving technology of the computer and video game industry. For a list of schools in the United States that offer degrees and course work in computer and video game design and programming, visit http://archives.igda.org/breakingin/resource_schools.php.

Competition for all types of programming jobs is increasing and will limit the opportunities of those people with less than a bachelor's degree.

Certification or Licensing

No specific certification is available for graphics programmers. General computer-related certifications are available from the Institute for Certification of Computing Professionals, whose address is listed at the end of this article. Although it is not required, certification may boost your attractiveness to employers during the job search.

Other Requirements
Successful graphics programmers need a high degree of reasoning ability, patience, and persistence, as well as an aptitude for mathematics and an artistic eye. They should also have strong writing and speaking skills, so that they can communicate effectively with coworkers and supervisors.

In the computer and video game industry, the work can be stressful, unpredictable, and demanding, so flexibility, enthusiasm, and a love for computer and video games are especially important.

EXPLORING

If you are interested in becoming a graphics programmer in the computer and video game industry, it is a good idea to start early and get some hands-on experience operating and programming a computer. One of the most obvious (and fun) ways to become familiar with the various genres and products of the computer and video game industry is to play lots of different types of computer and video games.

A trip to the local library or bookstore is likely to turn up books on computer programming in general, as well as computer and video game programming. Joining a computer club and reading professional magazines are other ways to become more familiar with this career field. In addition, you should explore the Internet, a great source of information about computer-related careers and the computer and video game industry. One source you might want to check out is *Computer Graphics,* a publication of the Special Interest Group on Computer Graphics. You can read back issues of this publication online at http://www.siggraph.org/publications. The group also offers a conference that high school students who are interested in computer graphics can attend. You also might want to read the online resource "Breaking In: Preparing For Your Career in Games," which is available at the International Game Developers Association's Web site (http://archives.igda.org/breakingin). The publication offers an overview of programming careers, profiles of workers in the field, and other resources.

Another way to gain experience is to visit a company that produces computer and video games and make an appointment to talk with one of the graphics programmers on the staff. You can also contact the computer science department of a local university to get more information about the field. It may be possible to speak with a faculty member whose specialty is computer graphics, or to sit in on a computer graphics class.

If you are interested in the artistic applications of graphics, get involved with artistic projects at school, like theater set design, poster and banner design for extracurricular activities, and yearbook or literary magazine design.

EMPLOYERS

Graphics programmers in the computer and video game industry typically work for small, independent game development studios, large computer and video game publishers, or manufacturers of the various computer and video game platforms. These companies are usually located in major cities, especially on the East and West Coasts. Major entertainment software publishers include Electronic Arts, Activision Blizzard, THQ, Nintendo of America, Atari, Sony, Take-Two Interactive Software, Microsoft, and Konami Digital Entertainment-America.

Graphics programmers in general are employed throughout the United States. Opportunities are best in large cities and suburbs where business and industry are active. Graphics programmers who develop software systems work for software manufacturers, many of which are in central California. There is also a concentration of software manufacturers in Boston, Chicago, and Atlanta. Programmers who adapt and tailor the software to meet specific needs of clients are employed around the country by the end users. Graphics programmers can also work in service centers that furnish computer time and software to businesses. Agencies, called job shops, employ programmers on short-term contracts. Self-employed graphics programmers can also work as consultants to small companies that cannot afford to employ full-time programmers.

STARTING OUT

You can look for an entry-level programming position in the computer and video game industry in the same way as most other jobs; there is no special or standard point of entry into the field. Individuals with the necessary qualifications should apply directly to companies or agencies that have announced job openings through a school's career services office, an employment agency, or the classified ads. As employers become increasingly selective about new hires and seek to hold down the costs of in-house training, internships in computer programming are a great opportunity—not only for on-the-job experience, but also for a possible position after graduation from college.

Any previous experience with writing code for games is worth mentioning on your resume, cover letter, and in interviews. Even if it was for a school project, or something done on your own time for fun, it still counts as experience. It shows what you are capable of doing as well as your potential, demonstrates your motivation, and may help you get your foot in the door at a game company.

One thing to keep in mind when looking for employment in the computer and video game industry is geographical location. While there are game companies in most major cities, most are located in cities on the East or West Coasts, in cities such as San Francisco, Seattle, and New York. You may need to consider relocating to boost your chances of finding a job in the computer and video game industry.

ADVANCEMENT

Programmers are often ranked by such terms as *entry-level, associate, junior,* or *senior programmers.* These titles are based on education, experience, and level of responsibility. After programmers have attained the highest available programming rank, they can choose to make other career moves in order to advance further. Some graphics programmers may wish to become a *lead programmer.* These programmers typically are in charge of a group of programmers working together on a computer game. In addition to being top-notch programmers, they also need to know how to manage a team of programmers (including those with specialties other than graphics programming), deal with upper-level management, and interact with other departments that contribute to the development of a game. These programmers need to have excellent interpersonal skills and enjoy motivating others to perform hard work and strive for excellence. Other management options a programmer might choose to pursue include director, vice president, or other upper-level administrative positions in the computer and video game industry. However, as the level of management responsibilities increases, the amount of technical work performed decreases, so management positions are not for everyone.

Because technology changes so rapidly, programmers must continuously update their training by taking courses sponsored by their employers or software vendors. For skilled workers who keep up to date with the latest technology, the prospects for advancement are good. As employers increasingly contract out programming jobs, more opportunities should arise for experienced programmers with expertise in specific areas to work as consultants.

In general, programming provides a solid background in the computer industry. Experienced programmers enjoy a wide variety of possibilities for career advancement in many computer-related fields.

EARNINGS

The U.S. Department of Labor reports that computer programmers earned median annual salaries of $69,620 in 2008. The lowest paid 10 percent of programmers earned less than $40,080 annually, and at the other end of the pay scale, the highest paid 10 percent earned more than $111,450 that same year. Computer programmers employed by software developers had mean annual earnings of $83,340. According to the International Game Developers Association, computer programmers employed in the computer and video game industry earn salaries that range from $55,000 (for a programmer with one or two years of experience) to $85,000 (for a lead programmer). The average salary for programmers employed in this industry is $62,500. Top salaries in this industry may reach as high as $300,000.

Programmers who work as independent consultants earn high salaries, but their salaries may not be regular. Overall, those who work for private industry earn the most.

Graphics programmers usually receive full benefits, such as health insurance, paid vacation, and sick leave.

WORK ENVIRONMENT

Most graphics programmers work with state-of-the-art equipment. They may work alone or as part of a team and often consult with the end users of the graphics program, as well as engineers and other specialists. They usually put in eight to 12 hours a day and work a 40- to 60-hour week. To meet deadlines or finish rush projects, they may work evenings and weekends and average 65 to 80 hours of work a week. At some companies, programmers sometimes find themselves working more than 24 hours at a time, so the office areas are set up with sleeping couches and other areas where employees can relax. Due to long workdays, deadline pressure, and job instability, the computer and video game industry can be a stressful environment in which to work.

Graphics programmers usually work in one primary location but sometimes travel to attend seminars, conferences, and trade shows. Programmers who work for software manufacturers may need to travel to assist current clients in their work or to solicit new customers for the software by demonstrating and discussing the product with potential buyers.

OUTLOOK

Overall, the U.S. Department of Labor predicts that employment for computer programmers is expected to decline slowly through 2016. Technological developments have made it easier to write basic code, eliminating some of the need for programmers to do this work. More sophisticated software has allowed more and more end users to design, write, and implement their own programs. As a result, many of the programming functions are transferred to other types of workers. In addition, programmers will continue to face increasing competition from international programming businesses where work can be contracted out at a lower cost.

However, the specialty of graphics programming should still have a promising future—especially in the computer and video game industry. As more applications for computer graphics are explored and businesses find ways to use graphics in their everyday operations, graphics programmers will be in demand. Since the field of graphics programming in the computer and video game industry is constantly changing, programmers should stay abreast of the latest technology to remain competitive.

FOR MORE INFORMATION

For industry information, contact the following organizations:
Academy of Interactive Arts and Sciences
23622 Calabasas Road, Suite 220
Calabasas, CA 91302-4111
Tel: 818-876-0826
http://www.interactive.org

Entertainment Software Association
575 Seventh Street, NW, Suite 300
Washington, DC 20004-1611
Email: esa@theesa.com
http://www.theesa.com

For information on careers and education, student memberships, and to read Careers in Computer Science and Computer Engineering, *contact*
IEEE Computer Society
2001 L Street NW, Suite 700
Washington, DC 20036-4910
Tel: 202-371-0101
Email: help@computer.org
http://www.computer.org

For information on certification, contact
Institute for Certification of Computing Professionals
2400 East Devon Avenue, Suite 281
Des Plaines, IL 60018-4629
Tel: 800-843-8227
http://www.iccp.org

For career advice and industry information, contact
International Game Developers Association
19 Mantua Road
Mt. Royal, NJ 08061-1006
Tel: 856-423-2990
http://www.igda.org

For industry information, contact
Software and Information Industry Association
1090 Vermont Avenue, NW, 6th Floor
Washington, DC 20005-4095
Tel: 202-289-7442
http://www.siia.net

For information on membership, conferences, and publications, contact ACM SIGGRAPH.
Special Interest Group on Computer Graphics (SIGGRAPH)
Association for Computing Machinery (ACM)
Two Penn Plaza, Suite 701
New York, NY 10121-0701
Tel: 212-626-0613
http://www.siggraph.org

Intellectual Property Lawyers

OVERVIEW

Intellectual property (IP) *lawyers* in animation-related industries focus on the protection of creative thought. Intellectual property lawyers may work with copyrights to protect works their clients have authored; trademarks to protect brand names and symbols associated with their clients' businesses; and patents to protect their clients' inventions and discoveries. IP attorneys may also work with companies to protect their trade secrets. IP lawyers in animation-related industries have been kept busy with the explosion of new games and platforms, as well as new technology used to create games, animated films, and commercials. It is their job to protect emerging new ideas and creations, such as a new game platform, a new game engine, a new type of software that is used to help create an animated movie, or a new computer and video game design. According to the Franklin Pierce Law Center, the United States is the largest producer of intellectual property in the world.

HISTORY

The concept of intellectual property is not a recent development—people have sought help to protect their ideas since the 1700s. Unfortunately, in the past both lawyers and clients were often frustrated in their attempts to gain support for patents and copyrights in court. The country as a whole, the court system, and Congress were intent on not allowing monopolies to gain control of innovative products or ideas. This fear of monopolization caused the patent holder to get little if any help or protection from the government. Within the past three decades, however, Congress and judges have started to see innovative ideas and products as valuable for our trade status in the international marketplace.

Attitudes are not the only things that have changed. Compared to the earliest years of inventions, innovative ideas, and patent seeking, huge amounts of intellectual property are now created and need protection daily. Intellectual property in animation-related industries now includes music, computer software, written documents like user manuals, programming code, game engines, graphics, and much more.

This boom in intellectual property and its need for protection have increased the demand for IP lawyers. Previously, IP law was a smaller segment of a law firm's business, so it was hired out to smaller, boutique-type law firms. Now major law firms, film and television studios, game development studios, computer and video game publishers, and manufacturers of the various computer and video game platforms have entire teams in-house to meet the demands of intellectual law.

THE JOB

Intellectual property lawyers in animation-related industries work with a wide variety of clients. For example, lawyers in the computer and video game industry work with individual programmers or game designers or those at the highest levels of management of a large game publisher. Those employed by animation studios work closely with animators, producers, directors, designers, and top executives. Those who work for corporations are usually in-house counsels concerned with decisions affecting the use of intellectual property within the company—common examples include game design, game engines, programming code, music rights, music and sound effects, graphics, platforms, and any technological discoveries. A video game itself is an example of intellectual property, but it also comprises many different elements that are also examples of intellectual property, and which might be owned by more than one person, group, or company. The most recognized categories of intellectual property are copyrights, trademarks, patents, and trade secrets.

Copyrights initially existed to protect "original works of authorship." This includes works of literature, music, and art. Copyright is now one of the most common forms of intellectual property protection in animation-related industries. Using a finished computer game as an example, the game itself can be copyrighted. Many other aspects of the game can be copyrighted as well, including the game plot, all of the programming code used in the game, and the musical components of the game. Copyright also is a major practice issue in the television and film industries. Pirated versions of animated films and television shows are often sold illegally to the public; this is a violation of copyright law. An animated character, such as Mickey Mouse or Bart Simpson, may be used illegally in print, online, and other settings, and it is the job of the intellectual property lawyer to help protect the legal rights of the company regarding these characters. In such instance, they might first contact the offending party by registered letter, asking them to cease and desist from using the character in any manner. If the party is unwilling to stop using the character at its Web site, in print advertising materials, or another setting, the lawyer may file a civil suit against the party to force it to stop using the character and, in many instances, seek financial compensation for copyright infringement.

Trademark rights involve the right to protect name recognition with the public. Trademarks can be many things. In a video game, for example, it can include the game name and any logo associated with it, names of characters in the game, and any unique weapons found in the game.

Patents are granted for the invention of something that is new, useful, and original. Editing or control functions, program languages, and core proprietary technology are examples of the aspects of a video game that may be patented. Examples of patents for animated films that have been filed with the United States Patent and Trademark Office include the method of creating animated motion pictures (1939), the means and method for producing animated cartoons (1961), and the method for the creation of a combined live-action and animation motion picture (1987).

Trade secrets are information that gives a company an advantage over their competition that doesn't fit into the other three categories. Examples of trade secrets include object, source, and machine code; techniques or methods used to create special effects in a game or animated film or television show; and business or marketing plans for a company.

IP lawyers have the task of protecting a client's creative interests, whether those interests are to patent a new product, or to ensure that a copyright hasn't been infringed upon. IP lawyers may work in all areas of intellectual property law; however, many lawyers specialize in copyright, patent, trademark, or licensing law. Whichever area the IP attorney focuses on, some job duties are the same across the board. One of the IP lawyer's main tasks is to counsel clients. Usually this counseling concerns whether the intellectual property can be copyrighted, patented, or trademarked; the best method of protection for the individual property; and whether the product or idea being discussed will infringe on someone else's copyright, patent, or trademark. They are often called upon to review advertising copy, press releases, and other official documents to ensure that there are no intellectual property problems. Another major task for an IP lawyer is the drafting of legal documents, such as patent applications and licensing agreements. They may also help their clients choose an Internet domain name or a trademark.

The IP lawyer also serves clients by being their advocate before administrative bodies and courts. The IP lawyer's goal is to secure the rights of the client and then protect those rights if others violate them. Conversely, if the IP lawyer's client is accused of violating someone else's intellectual property rights, the IP lawyer defends the client.

If a client believes his or her rights to intellectual property have been infringed upon, the IP attorney must try to prove that someone else has taken or used the client's intellectual property without consent. On the other hand, if a client is accused of infringing on another's intellectual property rights, the lawyer must try to prove that the item in question didn't deserve a copyright, patent, or trademark in the first place or that the protection is invalid. Although lawsuits are commonplace today, most IP lawyers consider litigation to be the last step and try to settle differences outside the courtroom.

REQUIREMENTS

High School

Because intellectual property often deals with creations in the scientific, engineering, literary, film and television, and music worlds, a background in any of those areas will be helpful. If you are interested in working as an IP lawyer in the computer and video game industry, you should take as many computer classes as you can while in high school. If you want to work in the film and television industries, courses in broadcasting, computer science, animation, and film studies will be useful. Additionally, anyone interested in any area of IP law should take courses in business, accounting, English, and government as well.

Postsecondary Training

As in other areas of law, IP lawyers most often complete an undergraduate degree and then graduate from law school. For most types of intellectual property law, the undergraduate degree does not have to have a special focus. The exception to that is patent law. If you want to become a patent lawyer, you should major in science, engineering, or physics. Other technology-related courses will also be helpful.

To apply to almost any law school, you must first pass the Law School Admission Test (LSAT). The LSAT is an aptitude test that is used to predict how successful an individual will be in law school. Most law schools teach courses in intellectual property law, but some have IP sections and degrees, such as Columbia University School of Law, Franklin Pierce Law Center, and George Mason University Law School.

Certification or Licensing
After graduating from law school, you will be eligible to take the bar exam in any state. After passing the bar, you will be sworn in as an attorney and will then be eligible to practice law. Patent attorneys who practice patent law before the United States Patent Office must go a step further and obtain additional certification. Would-be patent lawyers must pass the patent bar exam. According to the American Bar Association, you must hold a bachelor's degree in engineering, physics, or one of the sciences, hold a bachelor's degree in another subject, or have passed the Engineer in Training test in order to be eligible to take the patent bar exam.

Other Requirements
IP lawyers should have excellent written and oral communication skills. In fact, the American Bar Foundation says a recent survey shows that law firms are more interested in these skills than the overall legal knowledge of the interviewee. Also, having command of foreign languages is crucial because IP lawyers work with products and ideas in international markets. IP lawyers in the computer and video game industry should have a good understanding of computer and video games and their components. Those interested in working in the television and film industries should be knowledgeable about the technology that is used to create animated features, shorts, or commercials.

EXPLORING

IP law in an animation-related industry is a perfect career for someone who is interested in both science and technology and law. Because of this duality, you can explore the career by focusing on the legal side or on the science/technology side. To get experience on the legal side, seek summer jobs and internships with law offices where you live. You may be able to get a part-time job as a legal assistant. Any experience you can get writing technical or legal documents can also help, so don't rule out temporary jobs in any kind of business office. Also check out your local business college for special prelaw programs that offer introductory law courses to the public. If you can't get any hands-on experience right away, ask your school counselor for help in setting up a tour of a local law office or arranging for an interview with a law professional. To get experience in the science/technology side of animation-related industries, you can ask for a tour of a game company or animation studio, or you can arrange for an interview with a professional in the industry. You can also join your school's computer or animation club and check out related resources at your local library and on the Internet.

EMPLOYERS

Intellectual property lawyers are in high demand with many types of employers in the computer and video game industry. IP lawyers are employed at law firms, hardware manufacturing corporations, design studios, and software publishers. IP lawyers may also own their own businesses.

Intellectual property lawyers employed in the motion picture and television industries work for animation studios, television and film studios that have animation divisions, and related employers.

The main employer of IP attorneys outside of animation-related industries is the United States Patent and Trademark Office (USPTO), which is part of the Department of Commerce. The USPTO employs lawyers as trademark examiners, patent examiners, and more. Other departments in the government that employ IP lawyers include the Departments of Defense, Interior, Justice, and Energy. IP lawyers can also find employment in the United States Copyright Office.

Although IP lawyers are in high demand all over the country, most work in large cities where major corporations are headquartered. Other hot spots for IP lawyers include Washington, D.C., because of the government agencies located there, and the West Coast—like the Silicon Valley area in California and Los Angeles, California (where many film and television studios are located). Another hot spot is in and around Seattle—because of its concentration of computer and video game-related companies.

STARTING OUT

As in any area of law, internships and clerkships are usually the path to a quality job. For those interested in patent law specifically, applying for a clerkship in the United States Court of Appeals for the Federal Court in Washington, D.C., is a great way to gain experience. To apply for a part-time, unpaid internship during law school or soon after graduation, you should write directly to the court about six months in advance. To gain a full-time, paid clerkship position, law students should inquire sometime before the end of their second year. You can also apply for clerkships and internships with law firms. Another way to break into the IP law field is to get a job at the USPTO. Working directly with patents will put you in a better position for an IP job later in your career.

Most IP lawyers start out with internships and clerkships at firms or courts. In law firms or large corporate offices in animation-related industries, IP lawyers start out as low-rung associates and then advance as their experience and track records allow.

ADVANCEMENT

Associates with successful reputations and many years of experience can become partners in the law firm or advance within the legal department at a computer and video game company or animation studio. Whether in corporations, government agencies, or law firms, most IP lawyers, like other types of lawyers, are given more high-profile cases and more important clients as they become more experienced.

EARNINGS

According to the American Intellectual Property Law Association, the average salary for an IP attorney in corporate offices and patent firms is $119,000 per year. Inexperienced IP lawyers can expect to make between $80,000 and $85,000, and those with the most experience and success will earn more than $180,000 per year. The median income for partners in private law firms is over $200,000 per year, while associates' salaries are about $77,000. IP lawyers who own their own practices usually make $100,000 per year while salaries for those who work in law firms and corporations average slightly higher.

Salaries for all lawyers ranged from less than $54,460 to $166,400 or more in 2008, according to the U.S. Department of Labor.

Almost all corporations, firms, and government agencies provide medical insurance, vacation, sick days, and holidays. Partners in large firms can expect other perks as well, including company cars, spending allowances, bonuses, and more depending on the firm.

WORK ENVIRONMENT

IP attorneys, like lawyers in other areas, have heavy workloads and work long hours. IP lawyers employed by law firms, computer and video game companies, and animation studios may spend hours poring over documents with few breaks. Many law firms have weekly goals for their lawyers that include the number of hours billed to the client. Some of these goals can be extremely demanding. Most of the lawyer's time is spent indoors meeting with clients, researching, or arguing in court. Depending on their position in the company or firm, IP lawyers may lead a team of lawyers or supervise a group of paralegals and associates.

OUTLOOK

The outlook for intellectual property law is promising. This field is relatively new and the demand for IP professionals doesn't show signs of slowing. The growth of the computer industry and the Internet have provided a great amount of work for IP lawyers. As new computer software, animation technology, and online media enters the market, IP lawyers will be needed to protect it. According to the American Bar Association, even if other markets that use the services of lawyers are softened by recession, the demand for IP lawyers will remain high. Because there will always be a need to protect the creative resources of the people (such as computer and video games, animated films, and animation technology), there will also be a need for IP lawyers.

FOR MORE INFORMATION

For information on all areas of law, law schools, the bar exam, and career guidance, contact
American Bar Association
321 North Clark Street
Chicago, IL 60654-7598
Tel: 800-285-2221
Email: askaba@abanet.org
http://www.abanet.org/intelprop/home.html

To read the publications What Is a Patent, a Trademark and a Copyright? *and* Careers in IP Law, *visit the association's Web site.*
American Intellectual Property Law Association
241 18th Street South, Suite 700
Arlington, VA 22202-3419
Tel: 703-415-0780
Email: aipla@aipla.org
http://www.aipla.org

For computer and video game industry information, contact
Entertainment Software Association
575 Seventh Street, NW, Suite 300
Washington, DC 20004-1611
Email: esa@theesa.com
http://www.theesa.com

For career advice and industry information, contact
International Game Developers Association
19 Mantua Road
Mt. Royal, NJ 08061-1006
Tel: 856-423-2990
http://www.igda.org

For information on patent law, contact
National Association of Patent Practitioners
3356 Station Court
Lawrenceville, GA 30044-5674
Tel: 800-216-9588
http://www.napp.org

For information about intellectual property, job opportunities, and recent press releases, contact the USPTO. Its Web site offers a link designed specifically for creative students interested in invention and includes contest information.
United States Patent and Trademark Office (USPTO)
Office of Public Affairs
PO Box 1450
Alexandria, VA 22313-1450
Tel: 800-786-9199
Email: usptoinfo@uspto.gov
http://www.uspto.gov

Marketing Research Analysts

QUICK FACTS

School Subjects
Business
Mathematics

Personal Skills
Following instructions
Technical/scientific

Work Environment
Primarily indoors
Primarily one location

Minimum Education Level
Bachelor's degree

Salary Range
$33,770 to $102,143 to
$200,000

Certification or Licensing
Voluntary

Outlook
Faster than the average

DOT
050

GOE
13.02.04

NOC
N/A

O*NET-SOC
19-3021.00

OVERVIEW

Marketing research analysts in animation-related industries collect, analyze, and interpret data in order to determine potential demand for computer or video games or platforms or audience interest in animated films. By examining the buying habits, wants, needs, and preferences of consumers, research analysts are able to recommend ways to improve products, increase sales, and expand or market to customer bases.

HISTORY

Knowing what customers want and what prices they are willing to pay have always been concerns of manufacturers and producers of goods and services. As industries have grown and competition for consumers of manufactured goods has increased, businesses have turned to marketing research as a way to measure public opinion and assess customer preferences.

Marketing research formally emerged in Germany in the 1920s and in Sweden and France in the 1930s. In the United States emphasis on marketing research began after World War II. With a desire to study potential markets and gain new customers, U.S. firms hired marketing research specialists, professionals who were able to use statistics and refine research techniques to help companies reach their marketing goals. By the 1980s research analysts could be found even in a variety of Communist countries, where the quantity of consumer goods being produced was rapidly increasing. Today, the marketing research analyst is a vital part of the marketing team. By conducting studies and analyzing data, research professionals help companies address specific marketing issues and concerns.

Perhaps the first example of market research being put to use in the computer and game industry took place in the early 1970s. Nolan Bushnell released *Computer Space,* a video arcade game. Although based on the popular *Spacewar* game that had been floating around university mainframes for nearly a decade, it was a flop when released to the general public. The problem? The average person found it to be too complicated to play, and therefore not very entertaining. Taking this criticism into account, Bushnell made his next game, *Pong,* considerably simpler to play. The game quickly became popular and was a huge success.

Marketing computer and video game products has become more complicated as the industry continues to evolve and expand. The explosion of games available in different genres (action, adventure, simulation, and strategy, for example) has created specialty markets, each requiring different marketing techniques. Games that play on more than one platform also require different marketing tactics for each potential platform audience. Finally, with more and more companies producing similar games and platforms, the marketing emphasis now is on how to advertise a new product to set it apart from a similar product sold by a competitor, rather than just highlighting the product itself.

Marketing research in the motion picture and television industries has been conducted since the first movies were shown and television shows and commercials were broadcast. But it was not until animation became popular again in the 1980s as a result of technological innovations that large-scale research studies were conducted to determine viewer demographics, popular animation genres, and any other information that would help more viewers tune in to Saturday morning cartoon shows and encourage people to buy tickets to watch the latest animated feature. Today, market research techniques are used by all the major animation studios to devise marketing campaigns for animated films, television shows, and commercials, as well as animations that appear on the Internet.

THE JOB

Marketing research analysts collect and analyze all kinds of information in order to help game companies, educational software companies, animation studios, and advertising firms improve their products, establish or modify sales and distribution policies, and make decisions regarding future plans and directions. In addition, marketing research analysts are responsible for monitoring both in-house studies and off-site research, interpreting results, providing explanations of compiled data, and developing research tools. The emphasis placed on market research varies. In some companies, market research plays an enormous role—even dictating entirely which game ideas or animated films get developed and which ideas are killed. Other companies use market research in a more supportive role, using the information gathered to fine-tune current games in development or future game proposals or, in the instance of the motion picture industry, to assess audience demographics and related information.

One area of marketing research focuses on company products and services. In order to determine consumer likes and dislikes, marketing research analysts collect data on brand names, trademarks, product design, and packaging for existing products, items being test-marketed, and those in experimental stages. Analysts also study competing products and services that are already on the market to help game designers develop new products. In the motion picture and television industries, marketing researchers might study a competitor's animated films and marketing campaigns to learn what makes them successful.

In the sales methods and policy area of marketing research, analysts examine firms' sales records and conduct a variety of sales-related studies. For example, in the game industry information on game or platform sales in various geographical areas is analyzed and compared to previous sales figures, changes in population, and total and seasonal sales volume. By analyzing this data, marketing researchers can identify peak sales periods and recommend ways to target new customers. Such information helps marketers plan future sales campaigns and establish sales quotas and commissions.

Advertising research is closely related to sales research. Studies on the effectiveness of advertising in different parts of the country are conducted and compared to sales records. This research is helpful in planning future advertising campaigns, revising existing campaigns, and in selecting the appropriate media to use. For example, marketing researchers at Disney might gauge the effectiveness of a marketing campaign for a new animated film that is being conducted on the West Coast. If box office receipts are lower than expected, they might conduct additional marketing research to determine why the campaign was ineffective and revise the campaign in order to better reach potential moviegoers in other markets such as those on the East Coast.

Marketing research that focuses on consumer demand and preferences solicits opinions of the people who use the products or services being considered. Besides actually conducting opinion studies, marketing researchers often design the ways to obtain the information.

They write scripts for telephone interviews, develop direct-mail questionnaires and field surveys, and design focus group programs. In addition to these methods, analysts in animation-related industries often use communities, affinity groups, chat rooms, and forums to gather opinions and feedback regarding their products, as well as gamers' or viewers' preferences and habits in general. Communities involve assembling a group by setting up "meeting places" for users of a product to discuss their views and opinions. They can exist as online forums, online social networks, local gatherings (such as an advanced screening of an animated film), or a combination of the three. Chat rooms and online forums can be monitored by or even established by the market research analysts, and are great places to gather opinions and feedback regarding their products or an animated film.

Through one or a combination of these studies, market researchers are able to gather information on consumer reaction to the style, design, price, and use of a computer or video game or the interest of a potential demographic group (such as teens) in an animated film. This information is helpful for forecasting sales, planning design modifications, creating and adjusting advertising campaigns, and determining changes in features or content.

A number of professionals make up the marketing research team. The *project supervisor* is responsible for overseeing a study from beginning to end. The *statistician* determines the sample size—or the number of people to be surveyed—and compares the number of responses. The project supervisor or statistician, in conjunction with other specialists (such as *demographers* and *psychologists*), often determines the number of interviews to be conducted as well as their locations. *Field interviewers* survey people in various public places, such as shopping malls, movie theaters, office complexes, and popular attractions. *Telemarketers* gather information by placing calls to current or potential customers, to people listed in telephone books, or to those who appear on specialized lists obtained from list houses. Once questionnaires come in from the field, *tabulators* and *coders* examine the data, count the answers, code ambiguous answers, and tally the primary counts. The marketing research analyst then analyzes the returns, writes up the final report, and makes recommendations to the design team and/or management of the computer and video game company or animation studio.

Marketing research analysts must be thoroughly familiar with the products of their industry—for example a computer and video game, an animated feature film, a commercial, or a popular cartoon series on television or the Internet. They must also be thoroughly familiar with research techniques and procedures. Sometimes the research problem is clearly defined, and information can be gathered readily.

Other times, company executives may know only that a problem exists as evidenced by an unexpected decline in the sales of a game or platform or poor box office receipts. In these cases the market research analyst is expected to collect the facts that will aid in revealing and resolving the problem, using some of the many techniques and procedures at his or her disposal.

REQUIREMENTS

High School

Most employers require their marketing research analysts to hold at least a bachelor's degree, so a college preparatory program is advised. Classes in English, marketing, economics, mathematics, psychology, and sociology are particularly important. Courses in computing are especially useful, since a great deal of tabulation and statistical analysis is required in the marketing research field.

Postsecondary Training

A bachelor's degree is essential for careers in marketing research. Majors in marketing, business administration, statistics, computer science, history, or economics provide a good background for most types of research positions. In addition, course work in sociology and psychology is helpful for those who are leaning toward consumer demand and opinion research. Since quantitative skills are important in various types of industrial or analytic research, students interested in these areas should take statistics, econometrics, survey design, sampling theory, and other mathematics courses.

Many employers prefer that a marketing research analyst hold a master's degree as well as a bachelor's degree. A master's of business administration, for example, is frequently required on projects calling for complex statistical and business analysis. Graduate work at the doctorate level is not necessary for most positions, but it is highly desirable for those who plan to become involved in advanced research studies.

Certification or Licensing

The Marketing Research Association offers certification for marketing research analysts. Contact the association for more information.

Other Requirements

To work in this career, you should be intelligent, detail oriented, and accurate; have the ability to work easily with words and numbers; and be particularly interested in solving problems through data collection and analysis. In addition, you must be patient and persistent, since long hours are often required when working on complex studies.

As part of the market research team, you must be able to work well with others and have an interest in people. The ability to communicate clearly, both orally and in writing, is also important because you will be responsible for writing up detailed reports on the findings in various studies and presenting recommendations to management.

EXPLORING

You can find many opportunities in high school to learn more about the necessary skills for the field of marketing research in general. For example, experiments in science, problems in student government, committee work, and other school activities provide exposure to situations similar to those encountered by marketing research analysts.

You can also seek part-time employment as a survey interviewer at local marketing research firms. Gathering field data for consumer surveys offers valuable experience through actual contact with both the public and marketing research supervisors. In addition, many companies seek a variety of other employees to code, tabulate, and edit surveys; monitor telephone interviews; and validate the information entered on written questionnaires. You can search for job listings in local newspapers and on the Web or apply directly to research organizations.

If you want to work in the computer and video game industry, familiarizing yourself with computer and video games is one way to become aware of the industry, and thus the different aspects of a game or platform that a market research analyst might be concerned with. You can also inquire about *beta testing* new computer and video game products. Many companies provide information about beta testing on their Web sites. As a beta tester, you will be asked to play games currently in development and then critique the product. Your comments are then used to perfect the product before it is released to the general public. Another way to become involved in another aspect of computer and video game industry market research is to participate in *communities*—meeting places for users of a product to discuss their views and opinions. They exist as online forums, local gatherings, online social networks, or a combination of the three. These communities are frequently focused on one company or a specific product, often set up by the companies themselves to gather opinions and feedback regarding their products.

If you have an interest in working in the television or film industries, you should watch as many animated features and shorts as possible. You can learn why animated films such as *Shrek* and *Toy Story* were so popular, while others were less successful. You can also go to the Web sites of animation studios such as Pixar or Disney to read marketing materials for films, as well as learn about job opportunities in marketing that are available at these companies.

Another way to learn about opportunities in animation-related industries is to conduct an information interview with a marketing worker. Ask your school counselor to arrange an interview with a marketing professional who is employed by a game company or animation studio.

EMPLOYERS

In the computer and video game industry, marketing research analysts are typically employed by independent game development studios, computer and video game publishers, manufacturers of the various computer and video game platforms, and private research organizations that specialize in this industry. These companies are usually located in major cities, especially on the East and West Coasts. Major entertainment software publishers include Electronic Arts, Nintendo of America, Atari, Sony, Activision Blizzard, THQ, Take-Two Interactive, Microsoft, and Konami Digital Entertainment-America.

Marketing research analysts who are employed in the film and television industries work for independent producers, small and large animation studios, and film and television studios that have animation departments. Large animation companies include Pixar, Blue Sky Studios, Rhythm & Hues Studios, Lucasfilm Animation, Walt Disney Animation Studios, Warner Bros. Animation Studios, Sony Pictures Animation, and DreamWorks Animation SKG. Visit http://aidb.com for a database of thousands of animation-related companies.

While many marketing research organizations offer a broad range of services, some firms subcontract parts of an overall project out to specialized companies. For example, one research firm may concentrate on product interviews, while another might focus on measuring the effectiveness of product advertising. Similarly, some marketing analysts specialize in one industry, area, or platform.

Although many smaller firms located all across the country outsource studies to marketing research firms, these research firms, along with most large corporations that employ marketing research analysts, are located in big cities such as New York or Chicago.

In addition to working in animation-related industries, marketing research analysts are employed by large corporations, industrial firms, advertising agencies, data collection businesses, and private research organizations that handle local surveys for companies on a contract basis.

STARTING OUT

Students with a graduate degree in marketing research and experience in quantitative techniques have the best chances of landing jobs as marketing research analysts. Since a bachelor's degree in marketing or business is usually not sufficient to obtain such a position, many employees without postgraduate degrees start out as research assistants, trainees, interviewers, or questionnaire editors. In such positions, those aspiring to the job of market research analyst can gain valuable experience conducting interviews, analyzing data, and writing reports. In addition, many marketing positions in the computer and video game industry require some knowledge of computer games and platforms, and experience in the computer and video game industry. Working in computer and video game sales for a year or two is a good way to gain experience.

Use your college career services office and help wanted sections of local newspapers to look for job leads. The Internet also offers information on jobs and employers. If you are interested in working in the computer and video game industry, visit Web sites such as Animation World Network (http://www.awn.com), HighendCareers (http://www.highendcareers.com), GameJobs (http://www.gamejobs.com), Gamasutra (http://www.gamasutra.com), and Dice (http://www.dice.com). If you want to work in the film and television industries, your best bet is to contact animation studios directly or marketing firms that conduct research for these companies.

Another way to get into the marketing research field is through personal and professional contacts. Names and telephone numbers of potential employers may come from professors, friends, or relatives. Finally, students who have participated in internships or have held marketing research-related jobs on a part-time basis while in school or during the summer may be able to obtain employment at these firms or at similar organizations.

ADVANCEMENT

Most marketing research professionals begin as *junior analysts* or *research assistants*. In these positions, they help in preparing questionnaires and related materials, training survey interviewers, and tabulating and coding survey results. After gaining sufficient experience in these and other aspects of research project development, employees are often assigned their own research projects, which usually involve supervisory and planning responsibilities. A typical promotion path for those climbing the company ladder might be from assistant researcher to marketing research analyst to assistant manager and then to manager of a branch office for a large private research firm. From there, some professionals become market research executives or research directors for industrial or business firms.

Since marketing research analysts learn about all aspects of marketing on the job, some advance by moving to positions in other departments, such as advertising or sales. Depending on the interests and experience of marketing professionals, other areas of employment to which they can advance include data processing, teaching at the university level, statistics, economics, and industrial research and development.

In general, few employees go from starting positions to executive jobs at one company. Advancement often requires changing employers. Therefore, marketing research analysts who want to move up the ranks frequently go from one company to another, sometimes many times during their careers.

EARNINGS

Beginning salaries in marketing research depend on the qualifications of the employee, the nature of the position, and the size of the firm. Interviewers, coders, tabulators, editors, and a variety of other employees usually get paid by the hour and may start at $6 or more per hour. The U.S. Department of Labor reported that in 2008, median annual earnings of market research analysts employed in all industries were $61,070. Salaries ranged from less than $33,770 to more than $112,410. Experienced analysts working in supervisory positions at large firms can earn even higher earnings. Marketing research directors earn up to $200,000.

Game Developer magazine reports that marketing professionals in the computer and video game industry earned approximately $102,143 in 2008.

Marketing research analysts employed in the advertising industry earned mean annual salaries of $63,250 in 2008, while those employed by software publishers made $95,850. Because most marketing research workers are employed by business or industrial firms, they receive typical fringe benefit packages, including health and life insurance, pension plans, and paid vacation and sick leave.

WORK ENVIRONMENT

Marketing research analysts usually work a 40-hour week. Occasionally, overtime is necessary in order to meet project deadlines. Although they frequently interact with a variety of marketing research team members, analysts also do a lot of independent work, analyzing data, writing reports, and preparing statistical charts. In addition, those employed in animation-related industries often have a great deal of interaction with coworkers, such as with game and product designers in the computer and video game industry or with producers, art directors, and directors in the television and film industries.

Most marketing research analysts work in offices located at the firm's main headquarters. Others may work from home. Those who supervise interviewers may go into the field to oversee work. In order to attend conferences, meet with clients, or check on the progress of various research studies, many market research analysts find that regular travel is required.

OUTLOOK

The U.S. Department of Labor predicts that employment for marketing research analysts employed in all fields will grow faster than the average for all occupations through 2016. Increasing competition among computer and video game companies, strong sales of computer and video games (nearly 268 million games were sold in 2007, according to the Entertainment Software Association), and a growing awareness of the value of marketing research data will contribute to strong growth for game industry marketing research analysts. Opportunities will be best for those with a master's degree who also have previous experience with computer and video games. Employment for marketing managers in the film and television industries is expected to grow faster than the average for all careers. As more animated features are made, an increasing number of marketing professionals will be needed to help prepare marketing campaigns to reach the largest potential viewing audience. Employment for marketing research analysts employed in the advertising industry is expected to grow much faster than the average through 2016.

FOR MORE INFORMATION

For information on graduate programs, contact
American Association for Public Opinion Research
111 Deer Lake Road, Suite 100
Deerfield, IL 60015-4943
847-205-2651
Email: info@aapor.org
http://www.aapor.org

For career resources and job listings, contact
American Marketing Association
311 South Wacker Drive, Suite 5800
Chicago, IL 60606-6629
Tel: 800-262-1150
http://www.marketingpower.com

For career information, visit
Careers Outside the Box: Survey Research: A Fun, Exciting,
    Rewarding Career
http://www.casro.org/careers

For information on graduate programs in marketing, contact
Council of American Survey Research Organizations
170 North Country Road, Suite 4
Port Jefferson, NY 11777-2606
Tel: 631-928-6954
Email: casro@casro.org
http://www.casro.org

For industry information, contact the following organizations:
Entertainment Software Association
575 Seventh Street, NW, Suite 300
Washington, DC 20004-1611
Email: esa@theesa.com
http://www.theesa.com

Software and Information Industry Association
1090 Vermont Avenue, NW, 6th Floor
Washington, DC 20005-4095
Tel: 202-289-7442
http://www.siia.net

For comprehensive career information, including "Breaking In: Preparing For Your Career in Games," visit the IGDA Web site.
International Game Developers Association (IGDA)
19 Mantua Road
Mt. Royal, NJ 08061-1006
Tel: 856-423-2990
http://www.igda.org

For information on certification, education, and training, contact
Marketing Research Association
110 National Drive, 2nd Floor
Glastonbury, CT 06033-1212
Tel: 860-682-1000
http://www.mra-net.org

Modelers

QUICK FACTS

School Subjects
Art
Computer science
Mathematics

Personal Skills
Artistic
Communication/ideas

Work Environment
Primarily indoors
Primarily one location

Minimum Education Level
Associate's degree

Salary Range
$31,570 to $67,000 to
$100,390+

Certification or Licensing
None available

Outlook
About as fast as the average

DOT
N/A

GOE
N/A

NOC
5241

O*NET-SOC
27-1014.00

OVERVIEW

Animation, whether created by hand or computer-generated, begins with a sketch of an idea, animal, or character. The challenge of bringing this drawing "to life" is placed upon *modelers*. Using a variety of mediums or computer tools, modelers are able to transform a simple drawing into a complex model. Their work is often the first step in the creation of an animated character, environmental sets, or special effects. Modelers work with other animation team members in many different industries such as film, television, and computer and video gaming.

HISTORY

Modelers have played a role in the film industry ever since the first clay animation movies were made in the early 1900s. (Clay animation is an animation process in which objects or characters that are made of clay or another material are manipulated and filmed to suggest lifelike movement.) Modelers helped early animation filmmakers bring an artist's sketch to life in the form of a three-dimensional object.

Today, some modelers still use clay, latex, wire mesh, and other materials to create three-dimensional (3D) physical models for use in animation, but many use sophisticated software programs and other technologies to create computer-generated 3D animated objects. Although their tools and materials may have changed, modelers still have the same goal: creating realistic characters, objects, and backgrounds for animated films, commercials, medical simulations, and computer and video games.

THE JOB

Anyone who has watched claymation cartoons such as *Gumby* and *Wallace and Gromit,* and more recently, *Bob the Builder,* as well as computer-generated film favorites such as *Toy Story* and *Shrek,* has seen the work of modelers. None of these cartoons or feature films would be possible without the talent and creativity of modelers. Modelers work as part of a team of animators, art directors, and writers to bring a story to life. Using artists' storyboard sketches and the writer's script, modelers create a 3D version of a character, animal, or even background scenery or special effects; these objects and backgrounds are integral to the development of a cartoon or movie.

Modelers may use different approaches depending upon the task or their specialty. Some modelers build their geometric models using materials such as clay, latex, or wire mesh. A popular medium, one used for the *Gumby* claymation cartoon, for example, is a malleable substance known as plasticine clay. Modelers use sketches, plans, and descriptions created by artists and storywriters to shape a miniature 3D figure out of the clay or another material. This figure is then manipulated into a range of motions and poses, each captured on film, as dictated by the script. This process is known as *stop-motion*

A modeler poses with his current project, as well as with photos of the chicken-pie machine he created for the movie *Chicken Run. (Peter Clark, Newspix)*

animation. Modelers work closely with their animation team, the art director in particular, to make necessary changes in the body of the character or perhaps even their facial expressions. One or more modelers may be assigned to work on a project or particular character.

Many animated features today are created using computer-generated imagery. Modelers using this technique create their 3D models using graphics software programs such as Maya, form•Z, bonzai, 3ds Max, Softimage, LightWave, or Blender. The process is similar to that mentioned above, though instead of molding and sculpting 3D characters out of a physical material, modelers can create geometric structures on their computer screens. Storyboard artists and scriptwriters first create a simple depiction of the character. The *Toy Story* character Woody, for example, may have started out as various drawings of a cowboy doll. Modelers take these sketches and use computer technology to generate a basic wire or mesh figure before adding color, depth, and texture. Often modelers must redo or redesign their work as directed by animators, art directors, and technical directors assigned to the project until the character or object is approved. Approved model designs are then used by animators to create the action of the story. Even then, modelers are often asked to tweak certain aspects of the model to better work with the script. Some modelers may be assigned by art directors to create background characters, scenery, or even special effects needed to complete a film.

While many modelers are employed in the entertainment industry to help create cartoons and films, they may also find work creating 3D characters and effects for video games or the Web, medical models, or models of architectural designs.

REQUIREMENTS

High School
To prepare for this field, take art (including drawing), computer science, graphic design, and animation classes in high school. Math classes, such as algebra and geometry, will also be helpful. Many animation professionals today have college degrees, so you should take a college preparatory curriculum that includes history, government, and English.

Postsecondary Training
Many modelers have associate's or bachelor's degrees in fine arts or animation. Modelers who come from an architecture background might have degrees in engineering, architecture, or design. The Animation World Network offers a database of animation schools at its Web site (http://schools.awn.com). Another good source of schools

can be found at the International Game Developers Association's Web site (http://archives.igda.org/breakingin/resource_schools.php).

Other Requirements

To be a successful modeler, you must be highly creative and observant. You must be able to turn a two-dimensional sketch of a prop, environment, or character into a three-dimensional object by using art-oriented skills or computer technology. You must have knowledge of basic design principles such as balance, composition, shape/form, and rhythm. Modelers must also be able to follow instructions regarding the appearance of a model, and be able to accept constructive criticism if the item requires revision. You should also be able to work well on your own and be conscientious and organized about your work. The ability to meet deadlines is also important. Other key skills include curiosity, communication, adaptability, professionalism, and a willingness to learn throughout your career.

EXPLORING

One of the best ways to learn about this career is to actually try your hand at the work of a modeler. You can build models using clay, latex, wire mesh, and other materials or by using graphics software programs such as Maya, form•Z, or Blender to create 3D models. The goal is to experiment, learn new techniques, and have fun. If you are skilled enough to create something that impresses your friends or family—so much the better. You can also read books about animation modeling, visit Web sites about animation, and talk to a modeler about his or her career.

EMPLOYERS

Modelers are employed by animation, film, and television studios (such as Pixar, Walt Disney Animation Studios, and DreamWorks Animation SKG), computer and video game companies, advertising agencies, and architectural firms.

STARTING OUT

The best way to break into this field is by creating a demo reel of your work. The reel will give hiring managers an idea of your skills and creativity. It should be concise (four minutes or less in length) and feature only your best work.

Your college career services office may list job openings. Participation in an internship is a good way to gain hands-on experience, which employers like any new hire to have. Your college may require the completion of an internship as part of its requirement for graduation.

Conferences, such as the Game Developers Conference (http://www.gdconf.com), can provide you with job networking opportunities. Industry Web sites such as Animation World Network (http://www.awn.com), HighendCareers (http://www.highendcareers.com), GameJobs (http://www.gamejobs.com), Gamasutra (http://www.gamasutra.com), and Dice (http://www.dice.com) offer information on jobs and employers.

ADVANCEMENT

Modelers advance by working for larger companies or on more prestigious projects. For example, a modeler employed by a small animation company may one day gain enough skill and experience to get hired by Pixar, one of the most successful animation studios in the industry. Some modelers may become *art directors,* who lead entire production teams on projects. Others may continue their education and become animators or game designers.

EARNINGS

The U.S. Department of Labor does not provide salary information for the career of modeler. It does report that multimedia artists and animators earned salaries that ranged from less than $31,570 to $100,390 or more in 2008. Those employed in the motion picture and video industries had mean annual earnings of $71,910, while those who worked for software publishers earned $64,820. Contract modelers may make anywhere from $15-$150 an hour depending on the project.

Modelers who work full time for a company usually receive benefits such as vacation days, sick leave, health and life insurance, and a savings and pension program. Self-employed modelers must provide their own benefits.

WORK ENVIRONMENT

Modelers typically work in well-lighted offices or design studios. Their work environment is highly creative and filled with brainstorming sessions and a lot of give-and-take among coworkers and supervisors. One of the primary negatives of this profession is the long hours. Modelers typically work 50 hours or more a week and may work 80 or more hours a week when trying to meet deadlines.

OUTLOOK

The computer and video game industry and the film and television industry are continuing to enjoy strong growth as a result of increasing interest in games and animated films. This is generally good news for modelers, although jobs in these industries have recently been outsourced to companies in foreign countries that pay salaries that are less than those paid to workers in the United States. Modeling is one of the first skills taught in college programs, so many people have a basic knowledge of the field. As a result, it is extremely important for modelers to have the most up-to-date skill set and education in order to land a job.

FOR MORE INFORMATION

For industry information, contact
Entertainment Software Association
575 Seventh Street, NW, Suite 300
Washington, DC 20004-1611
Email: esa@theesa.com
http://www.theesa.com

For comprehensive career information, including "Breaking In: Preparing For Your Career in Games," visit the association's Web site.
International Game Developers Association
19 Mantua Road
Mt. Royal, NJ 08061-1006
Tel: 856-423-2990
http://www.igda.org

=========== **INTERVIEW** ===========

J. Cody Lucido is a 3D modeler and the owner of Codeman Studios LLC in Washington State. (Visit his Web site, http://www.code-manstudios.com, to learn more about his career and view samples of his work.) Cody discussed his career with the editors of Careers in Focus: Animation.

Q. What made you want to become a modeler?
A. I have always had a love of art and started painting and sculpting as a kid. One of my earliest inspirations was Ray Harryhausen from the Sinbad movies. I tried to make my own stop-motion movies and this led to sculpting the characters out of wire and

foam latex. Later in my career I worked at Hallmark Cards Inc. In Kansas City, Missouri, and took my sculpting to a new level by working on 3D products. I would sculpt the masters out of a proprietary wax and heated needle. About this time computers were running beta versions of Photoshop and other software. I dreamed of one day being able to sculpt on the computer as well. I followed the technology as it developed to the incredible place it is today.

Q. Can you tell me about Codeman Studios and describe a typical day on the job?

A. Codeman Studios is my umbrella place for all of my freelance projects. A typical day for me is to check out some of my favorite forums in the morning, then plan the day depending on the workload. If I have a major project going on it can easily consume 10–14 hours a day. When work is something you love the time melts by. Be sure to get up and move around!

Q. How did you train for this field?

A. I am self-taught. If there is something I want to learn to do I tend to obsess and research it until I can find out everything I can. I recommend the Web as an amazing resource for this and don't forget to join one of the many forums. You will be able to mix it up in most cases with professionals working in the field and most are very nice people willing to help a newbie.

Most importantly though is to just do it. Try and model something every day if you can. If you really want to be a modeler deep down, you will find the time. Also don't neglect your 2D skills. Draw, draw, draw! So often clients need to see a 2D representation before you take the plunge into 3D.

Q. What are the most important personal and professional skills for modelers?

A. While it is important as an artist to have a well-developed sense of ego, learn how to keep it in check and listen to input and criticism from your peers. This will be invaluable when working in a team environment, plus it will make you a better artist.

Keep as current as you can with not only style, but technique and software as well. This is a fast-moving field and there are constantly new innovations. The Internet will keep you updated.

As mentioned before do not let your 2D skills suffer in your pursuit of 3D. You will find this invaluable.

Be original while still meeting the requirements of the client. I work very hard to try and understand what the client's vision is. It is my job to help realize that. I often find that asking questions and offering ideas is a sure way to bring the client's vision to life and also put your own spin on it.

Do not undervalue your work, and don't work for free. Too many people think that if they give some work away for no pay they will be noticed. In my experience this is not true because the reality is if they come back to you they will want it free again or move on to another amateur who will give it away for free. Many people do this and it deflates the value of the work done by paid professionals.

Q. What is the employment outlook for modelers? What areas are growing? Declining?

A. The field is actually a relatively new one and so there is opportunity; however, with a glut of game schools cranking out semi-qualified people the opportunities are drying up. This mixed with the recent economic turns and the closing of many game houses have caused the market to be flooded by super talented artists. Newbies will find it hard to get a job unless they know someone or have amazing talent.

The advent of the 3D sweatshops in China, India, and Korea are also wreaking havoc on the U.S. market. They are probably the worst offenders for depleting jobs. Don't look for it to get better before it gets worse.

For me diversity is the key. Here is an example. I was offered a freelance job to draw the 2D orthographic views of game pieces for a child's board game. When I met the client I showed him that I could sculpt the pieces in 3D and then render as many orthos as he wanted for the same cost as 2D drawings. He loved it and I got the gig.

Producers

QUICK FACTS

School Subjects
Art
Business
Computer science

Personal Skills
Communication/ideas
Leadership/management

Work Environment
Primarily indoors
Primarily one location

Minimum Education Level
Bachelor's degree

Salary Range
$46,667 to $82,905 to
$125,000+

Certification or Licensing
None available

Outlook
Faster than the average

DOT
187

GOE
01.01.01

NOC
5121

O*NET-SOC
27-2012.00s

OVERVIEW

Producers are responsible for the completion of a project—from the initial funding to its final delivery. They may oversee the creation of a video game, a commercial, an animation simulation for the health care industry or military, a music video, or an animated film or television show. Their administrative duties include coordinating all talent, managing demands for equipment or supplies, and overseeing any staffing problems, in order to keep the project on schedule. They work closely with other producers and the director to make certain the project runs smoothly; they report to studio or game executives.

HISTORY

Motion picture cameras were invented in the late 1800s, and the first animated cartoon was created by Frenchman Émile Reynaud in 1892. *Fantasmagorie,* considered the first fully animated film, was made by French director Émile Courtet (aka Émile Cohl) in 1908. The creators of early animated films also served as producers—managing both creative and business elements of their works. This continued in the early decades of the 20th century.

It was not until the 1930s and 1940s—what many consider to be the golden age of animation—that producers began receiving separate credits for "producing" a movie. Despite the new job title, many of these producers were still actually the creators of the films or, like Walt Disney, even owners of animation studios.

Technological innovations created a renaissance in the animation industry in the late 1980s, which allowed a larger number of better-quality animated films and television shows to be released. Two examples include the movie *Who Framed Roger Rabbit?* (1988) and *The Simpsons* (a television show that debuted in 1989). The success of animated films and shows over the last three decades has created a need for producers to assemble and manage creative talents, locate project funding, oversee business operations, and ensure that animated films and shows are successful once they are released.

Producers also work in the computer and gaming industry—although their roots in this field can only be traced back to the early 1970s when Atari introduced *Pong*, the first mainstream video game. Since then, new consoles have come out, including some forgotten hits, such as Intellivision and Colecovision; to more recent names, such as Nintendo, Sega, Sony PlayStation, and Microsoft Xbox. The industry has become a billion-dollar venture, with much to win in the case of a hot game (think *Super Mario Brothers* in its heyday), but also much to lose in the case of a financial sinker (think *E.T. the Extra Terrestrial*—a game so unpopular it actually ended the life of the Atari 2600 console). Because of this financial risk, the job of producer was born, to oversee the creative people working away on the details of the game, while making sure the client and consumer interest would ensure a project was financially viable from the start and would be marketable in the future.

Books to Read for Aspiring Producers

Boyd, S. Gregory. *Business & Legal Primer for Game Development*. Florence, Ky.: Charles River Media, 2006.

Chandler, Heather Maxwell. *The Game Production Handbook*. Sudbury, Mass.: Jones & Bartlett Publishers, 2008.

Irish, Dan. *The Game Producer's Handbook*. Florence, Ky.: Course Technology PTR, 2005.

Jeffrey, Tom. *Film Business: A Handbook for Producers*. 3d ed. Crows Nest, NSW, Australia: Allen & Unwin, 2006.

Milic, Lea, and Yasmin McConville. *The Animation Producer's Handbook*. New York: Open University Press, 2006.

Muir, Shannon. *Gardner's Guide to Writing and Producing Animation*. Washington, D.C.: Garth Gardner Company, 2007.

Raugust, Karen. *The Animation Business Handbook*. Rev. ed. New York: St. Martin's Press, 2004.

THE JOB

Producers help create computer and video games; animated feature films, shorts, and commercials; and other products that feature animation. The following paragraphs provide more information on job responsibilities for producers by industry.

Computer and video game producers oversee and manage the development of video and computer games. While they do not generally handle the technical aspects of projects, they are responsible for coordination, management, and overall quality of the final product. At some companies, however, the producer will take on more technical duties, including serving as the lead designer. Most often, the producer is the liaison or "middle man" between the publisher and the game development team.

Producers must have widely varied knowledge of all aspects of the computer and video game industry. Whether their background is in computers, business, or art, producers must efficiently manage all steps of the development process. They assist the game development staff in the licensing of software, artwork, sound, and other intellectual properties.

Producers have many administrative duties, including scheduling meetings and managing documentation. They are also responsible for general business management duties, including hiring and firing of staff. It is essential that producers are excellent communicators given than they work with and manage all different types of personalities. There are two very different sides to the video game industry—the business side and the creative side. Both executive, financial-minded professionals and creative, art-minded professionals must communicate their ideas to the producer, who is then responsible for collaborating these ideas effectively.

Interactive line producers are specialized professionals who act as liaisons between producers and the production staff of interactive products such as computer and video games and online or wireless products. They supervise staff, financial budgets, and scheduling timelines.

Animation projects, large or small, need capable individuals to ensure that work gets done in a timely manner, staff is kept productive, and financial sponsors are happy. Depending on the size and scope of a project, there may be numerous producers assigned, each one responsible for a certain process or specialty. *Animation producers* oversee all aspects of an animation project from preproduction to postproduction stages. As the "go-to person" of a project, producers have the ultimate responsibility for making sure they deliver, in a timely manner, a finished product to the client, be it a major studio, advertising firm, or other businesses using animation sequences. Producers also drum up interest and secure financing for a project—whether from the studio, outside sources, or at times, their own investment. This is a challenging position, since producers must protect the vision of the directors and writers, while keeping aware of the time and financial limits of a project.

A producer's duties include interviewing and hiring a crew of artists, stylists, writers, animators, directors, editors, and other technical workers. Producers also plan and implement a schedule for filming and production, keeping aware of important deadlines, or addressing problems that may cause delays. On a daily basis, producers may meet with animators to view the samples of their work sequences, brainstorm with directors regarding creative ideas, meet with accounting staff to make sure the project is within set budgets, or meet with outside vendors to iron out details of merchandising, future DVD sales, or marketing and promotion strategies.

Producers may be responsible for overseeing several shows, episodes, or commercials in different stages of production. Depending on the scope of the project, there may be one or more individuals sharing the role of producer. Regardless of their industry, there are several specialized producer positions for workers in the field. The highest-level producing job is that of the *executive producer,* or *senior producer.* This individual trains, mentors, and manages other producers. The executive producer resolves project conflicts, and may have extended contact with clients. In addition to overseeing all other producers and workers on a project, the executive producer is responsible for obtaining funding, updating clients on the progress of projects, and eventually, submitting the final work to the client for approval.

Line producers serve as the liaison between the film's executive producers and the production staff. They spend a great deal of time in the editing room overseeing the daily progress of a project. In addition, line producers monitor scheduling and financial concerns, or staffing difficulties, and create solutions to these problems. They may also be called on to place orders with different vendors for technical products or supplies.

Associate producers provide administrative and technical support to executive producers of a project. This is often an entry-level position. They may help schedule meetings, organize schedules, research historical or technical details, and iron out any budget concerns. There may be one or more associate producers assigned to work on a project, especially for a major film or game project. In the computer and video game industry, associate producers' main responsibilities are overseeing research and product testing. They gather information for the development team, as well as oversee video game testers.

Associate producers may have authority over testers, but usually not over any other employees.

Assistant producers, who are also known as *production assistants,* serve as aides to higher level producers. This occupation is a step toward becoming a producer, but assistants do not usually have much, if any, decision-making authority.

REQUIREMENTS

High School

While an interest in playing video games is obviously a requirement if you want to work in the game industry, as a producer you will need to know a lot more about the technical side of game development and testing. For this reason, make sure you create a good foundation by taking math and computer science classes while in high school. Art classes are also useful to stimulate and develop your creative sensibilities, such as illustration—both by hand and with computer drawing tools.

High school courses that will be of assistance to you in your work as a motion picture or television producer include film, animation, speech, mathematics, business, psychology, and English.

Postsecondary Training

Most larger game developers will require not only its producers, but also its programmers, testers, and other entry-level workers, to have a college degree. Bachelor's degrees in computer science with an emphasis in programming or Web design are preferred, though many enter the industry with business degrees that can come in handy when dealing with clients, balancing the budget, and developing a strong business plan.

Those who are interested in working on animated films or shorts should undertake formal study of film, television, communications, theater, writing, English literature, or art. Many entry-level positions in the film industry are given to people who have studied liberal arts, cinema, or both.

In the United States there are more than a 1,000 colleges, universities, and trade schools that offer classes in film or television studies; more than 120 of these offer undergraduate programs, and more than 50 grant master's degrees. A small number of Ph.D. programs also exist.

Other Requirements

While degrees can help get you in the door of the larger companies, experience is what really counts in the gaming industry. If you are a high school graduate with years under your belt as a game tester, programmer, or production assistant, you might just get the job over a recent college graduate with no industry experience. Because the job of producer includes much administrative work, producers should have working knowledge of basic commercial software, such as Microsoft Office programs and FileMaker Pro. Familiarity with industry software used in game development is also often a requirement, since producers are heavily in the mix of designers, programmers, and testers.

Animation producers should have a keen knowledge of the animation industry and a keen sense for what projects will be artistically and commercially successful.

Communication and mediating skills are a must in this job, since producers are often forced to solve problems among staff members and make decisions based on varying opinions and priorities, such as those of the developer and those of the client.

EXPLORING

To explore a career in the computer and video game industry, make sure to cultivate your love of games and technology in general. To be able to manage game workers, sell an idea to a client, and make sure all parties are happy while the game is in the works, you had better love the product. But to cultivate this interest in video games doesn't necessarily mean you have to become a hermit with your PlayStation. Many schools and communities host computer science clubs that have special chapters catering to avid gamers. If you can't find such a club, start one with your friends. Schedule tournaments, discuss the best and worst games you've discovered, and think about what makes a game fly off the shelves. This is what a producer has to worry about every day at the office, while still maintaining a passion for playing. To learn more about the industry and its employers, visit the Web site of E3, the Electronic Entertainment Expo (http://www.e3expo.com), an annual trade show composed of computer and video game manufacturers from around the world. While the show is closed to the public, the site will give you an idea of what companies are out there.

If you want to work in the television or film industries, there are many ways to gain experience. Some high schools have animation clubs, for example, or courses on the use of animation software such as Flash. You can also read books about animation and visit the Web sites of animation associations and studios. One of the best ways to get experience is to make a short animated film of your own or get together with a group of friends to create an animated feature. You could assemble and manage the animation artists and brainstorm ways to get the film screened at a local animation festival once it's completed. This will help you learn about the challenges and rewards of producing an animated film.

EMPLOYERS

Computer and video game producers work for companies of all sizes. While the largest companies are located on the East and West Coasts and in Texas, Illinois, Maryland, and Massachusetts, smaller employers can be found almost anywhere in the country. Major entertainment software publishers include Activision Blizzard, Electronic Arts, Nintendo of America, Atari, Sony, THQ, Take-Two Interactive, Microsoft, and Konami Digital Entertainment-America.

Many producers in the film and television industries are self-employed. Others are salaried employees of film companies, television networks, and television stations. Approximately 1,700 motion picture, television, and new media producers are members of the Producers Guild of America—although all of these people do not work in animation. The greatest concentration of motion picture producers is in Hollywood and New York City. Large animation companies include Pixar, Blue Sky Studios, Rhythm & Hues Studios, Lucasfilm Animation, Walt Disney Animation Studios, Warner Bros. Animation Studios, Sony Pictures Animation, and Dream-Works Animation SKG. Visit http://aidb.com for a database of thousands of animation-related companies.

STARTING OUT

Because work experience is valued so highly in all animation-related industries, your best bet for landing your first job is with a small, start-up developer or animation studio. These companies may be more willing to hire less experienced workers in the hopes that they will stay on staff longer than an experienced (and more sought after) producer.

Jobs are easy to find online; most employers post job openings on their company Web sites or with large job search engines. However, because of the industry's popularity, many open positions do not remain open for long. Jobs often are filled internally or through connections before there ever is a need to post a job classified.

Those who want to work in the gaming industry should visit Web sites such as Animation World Network (http://www.awn. com), HighendCareers (http://www.highendcareers.com), GameJobs (http://www.gamejobs.com), Gamasutra (http://www.gamasutra.

com), and Dice (http://www.dice.com) for information on jobs and employers.

Those interested in producing animated films should approach film companies, television stations, or the television networks about employment opportunities. Positions may also be listed in trade publications and at the Web sites of professional associations, such as the Producers Guild of America (http://www2.producersguild. org/jobs).

ADVANCEMENT

The jobs of assistant producer or associate producer are entry-level positions. Advancement comes in the form of higher-level producing jobs—the top position being that of the executive producer, who is responsible for the entire project, beginning to end. Some producers become directors or make enough money to finance their own projects.

EARNINGS

Game Developer magazine reports that producers in the computer and video game industry earned approximately $82,905 in 2008. Associate producers with three or fewer years' experience earned an average salary of $46,667. Those with six or more years' experience earned $65,147. Producers/project leads with less than three years' experience earned an average salary of $62,500. Those with six or more years' experience earned $67,500. Executive producers with at least six years in the field earned average salaries of $125,000.

The Animators Guild Local 839, a union that represents animation professionals in California, conducts an annual survey of its members. It reports that producers earned weekly salaries that ranged from $1,500 to $3,605 in 2009.

The U.S. Department of Labor reports the following mean annual salaries for producers by industry in 2008: motion picture and video, $98,930; advertising; $107,520; and television broadcasting, $71,860.

Earnings vary based on skill, experience, and ability to produce high-quality, top-selling games or animated films on time and within budget.

Benefits for producers depend on the employer; however, they usually include such items as health insurance, retirement or 401(k) plans, and paid vacation days. Self-employed producers must provide their own benefits.

WORK ENVIRONMENT

Producers work in bustling, hectic environments that may be viewed as exciting to some, but stressful to others. To succeed at this job, producers need to be able to juggle many tasks at once and work with varying personalities, from creative professionals and technical workers, to the client whose only interest may be the bottom line. Balancing these (often opposing) priorities can make for a trying, but also exciting, work environment.

OUTLOOK

According to a 2004 survey conducted by the Entertainment Software Association, 53 percent of game players interviewed predicted that in 10 years they would play video games as much or even more than they do now. This increasing demand for challenging and entertaining games creates a steady job market for computer and video game producers. Overall, employment in this job should grow faster than the average for all careers through the coming decade. One caveat: This is a very popular industry. Talented, artistic, business-minded individuals will be drawn to the business of making and selling computer and video games, causing an influx of applicants for limited numbers of jobs. Individuals with more experience will find it the easiest to find jobs. However, with the industry's growth, individuals who are hard working, flexible, and passionate about gaming should be able to find entry-level jobs in computer and video game production.

Employment for producers employed in the motion picture and video industries is expected to grow about as fast as the average for all careers through 2016, according to the U.S. Department of Labor. Though opportunities may increase with the expansion of cable and satellite television, video and DVD rentals, online rental and purchase options, and an increased overseas demand for American-made animated films and television shows, competition for jobs will be high. Some positions will be available as current producers leave the workforce. Employment for producers employed in the advertising industry is also expected to grow about as fast as the average through 2016.

FOR MORE INFORMATION

IGDA offers professional and academic advice, including information on scholarships. Be sure to check out "Breaking In: Preparing for

Your Career in Games," an online guide covering different careers in the visual arts and interviews with top workers in the field.

International Game Developers Association (IGDA)
19 Mantua Road
Mt. Royal, NJ 08061-1006
Tel: 856-423-2990
http://www.igda.org

The guild is the leading professional organization for film and television producers. Visit its Web site for information about career options and to view profiles of producers.

Producers Guild of America
http://www.producersguild.org

This nonprofit organization represents "visual effects practitioners including artists, technologists, model makers, educators, studio leaders, supervisors, public relations/marketing specialists, and producers in all areas of entertainment from film, television and commercials to music videos and games." Visit its Web site for information about festivals and presentations and news about the industry.

Visual Effects Society
5535 Balboa Boulevard, Suite 205
Encino, CA 91316-1544
Tel: 818-981-7861
Email: info@visualeffectssociety.com
http://www.visualeffectssociety.com

Scriptwriters

QUICK FACTS

School Subjects
Business
English

Personal Skills
Artistic
Communication/ideas

Work Environment
Primarily indoors
Primarily one location

Minimum Education Level
High school diploma

Salary Range
$28,020 to $75,000 to
$117,602+

Certification or Licensing
None available

Outlook
Faster than the average

DOT
131

GOE
01.01.02

NOC
5121

O*NET-SOC
27-3043.00, 27-3043.02

OVERVIEW

Scriptwriters write scripts for computer and video games (such as *Halo, Guitar Hero,* and *Super Mario Galaxy*), animated films (such as *WALL-E, Happy Feet,* or *Bolt*), television shows (such as *Johnny Test* or *The Simpsons*), commercials, and animated training simulations or other products that are used in the military and a wide variety of industries (including health care and education). Other scriptwriters write non-animated dramas, comedies, soap operas, adventures, westerns, documentaries, newscasts, and training films. Scriptwriters may choose themes themselves, or they may write on a theme assigned by a producer or director. Scriptwriting is an art, a craft, and a business. It is a career that requires imagination and creativity, the ability to tell a story using both dialogue and pictures, and the ability to negotiate with producers and studio executives. Scriptwriters are sometimes called *screenwriters.*

HISTORY

Émile Reynaud, a French science teacher, created what is considered the first animated cartoon in 1892. But *Talkartoons,* the first cartoon series that had dialogue, was not released until 1930, according to *Animation Art: From Pencil to Pixel, the History of Cartoon, Anime, and CGI.* The series featured the cartoon character Betty Boop, who is still popular today. In the 1930s Walt Disney began focusing on improving storytelling techniques in his cartoon shorts; other animators followed his lead. In 1937 he released *Snow White and the Seven Dwarfs,* which many consider to be the first feature-length animated film. At 83 minutes in length, *Snow White* featured a large amount of dialogue that had to ring true and move the story along. The story itself was adapted from a fairy tale by the Brothers Grimm. Walt Disney and other animators at his studio were responsible for writing the dialogue; the position of "animation scriptwriter" was not yet a separate job title in the animation world. Today, scriptwriters are distinct professionals in the motion picture and television industry (although animators, directors, and other creative professionals also often contribute to a script for an animated project). Scriptwriters are paid top dollar to write or adapt screenplays for animated films, television series, animated commercials, and any other animation project that requires a script.

The computer and video game industry developed in the 1960s and 1970s, but it wasn't until the creation of more complex and multifaceted games in the mid-to-late 1990s that writers became an integral part of the creation of actual video and computer games. Today's writers create the plot, story lines, dialogue (known as "barks"), and voice-overs for computer and video games. As games companies continue to compete for market share in this highly competitive industry, these professionals will be increasingly relied on to give each game an extra edge.

THE JOB

Computer and Video Game Industry

Scriptwriters create the plot, story lines, dialogue, and voice-overs for computer and video games. Unlike movie or television scriptwriting, writing a video game does not typically involve a linear plot, but rather a plot that contains multiple and expanding branches and many different outcomes, depending on the skill and actions of the game player. Scriptwriters who focus on interrelated dialogue are called *interactive conversation writers*. Scriptwriters must be keenly aware of every possibility that can occur in a game and write dialogue and plot lines that match these possibilities. They need to understand basic character development, context setting, and backstory and setting design. Scriptwriters must also have a strong knowledge of the background and history of the game for which they are writing content. For example, a scriptwriter creating content for a game set in Europe during World War II would need to have knowledge of (or be able to research) British and American military lingo; the weapons, vehicles, and other equipment used during the war; the history of Allies and Axis countries during that time span; and other facts about this conflict. Scriptwriters work closely with game designers to ensure that their writing and the technical pacing of the game are in sync. Unless they also have experience as game programmers, scriptwriters do not usually participate in the initial planning stages of a game, but are hired on a contract basis after the game idea has been approved.

Animated Films, Television Shows, and Commercials

Scriptwriters write scripts for continuing television series such as *The Simpsons, Dora the Explorer,* and *South Park;* animated films such as *Ratatouille, Kung Fu Panda,* or *Persepolis;* animated shorts that appear on the Internet; television commercials that feature animation; and training software that is used in a variety of industries. Scriptwriters may write original stories or copy, or get inspiration from newspapers, magazines, books, video games, or other sources.

Film and television scripts are written in a two-column format, one column for dialogue and sound, the other for action instructions. Screenwriters send a query letter outlining their idea before they submit a script to a production company. Then they send a standard release form and wait at least a month for a response. Studios buy many more scripts than are actually produced, and studios often will buy a script only with provisions that the original writer or another writer will rewrite it to their specifications.

Scriptwriters may work on a staff of writers and producers for a large company. Or they may work independently for smaller companies that hire only freelance production teams. Advertising agencies also hire writers, sometimes as staff, sometimes as freelancers.

REQUIREMENTS

High School

You can develop your writing skills in English, theater, speech, and journalism classes. Belonging to a debate team can also help you learn how to express your ideas within a specific time allotment and framework. History, government, and foreign language can contribute to a well-rounded education, necessary for creating intelligent scripts. A business course can be useful in understanding basic business principles you will encounter when dealing with contracts, rights, and related issues. Experience with animation and computer and video games will also be useful.

Postsecondary Training

There are no set educational requirements for scriptwriters. A college degree is desirable, especially a liberal arts education, which exposes you to a wide range of subjects. An undergraduate or graduate film program will likely include courses in screenwriting, film theory, and other subjects that will teach you about the film industry and its history. A creative writing program will involve you with workshops and seminars that will help you develop fiction writing skills. Those who want to work in the game industry should take classes in computer and video game-related topics.

Many colleges and universities have film departments that offer screenwriting programs, but some of the most respected film schools are the University of California-Los Angeles (http://www.tft.ucla.edu/ftv_mfa), the University of Southern California (http://www-cntv.usc.edu/programs/writing), the American Film Institute (http://www.afi.com), and Columbia University (http://wwwapp.cc.columbia.edu/art/a pp/arts/film/index.jsp). Contact these schools or visit their Web pages for information about course work and faculty.

Other Requirements

As a scriptwriter, you must be able to create believable characters and develop a story. You must have technical skills, such as dialogue writing, creating plots, and doing research. In addition to creativity and originality, you also need an understanding of the marketplace for your work. You should be aware of what kinds of scripts are in demand by producers (or, if you work in the game industry, what type of games are currently popular). Word processing skills are also helpful.

Varied interests and curiosity are also important for screenwriters. One day you might be researching the slang used in the Wild West in the 1880s and the next social customs of Confucian China. If you are creating a futuristic video game or animated film or show, you will have to use your creativity to imagine how people of the future will talk and act.

In addition to the stress caused by the instability of working on a freelance basis, there's a lot of stress in the work itself. Scriptwriters must meet constant deadlines. And because the process requires a great deal of collaboration, they must be ready to throw away something they have just spent a great deal of time writing if others in their team have a different approach.

EXPLORING

One of the best ways to learn about scriptwriting is to read and study scripts. It is advisable to watch an animated feature such as *Shrek* or *WALL-E* while simultaneously following the script. You should read film-industry publications, such as *Daily Variety* (http://www.

variety.com), *Hollywood Reporter* (http://www.hollywoodreporter.com), and *Hollywood Scriptwriter* (http://www.hollywoodscriptwriter.com). There are a number of books about screenwriting. Some offer an inside look at the world of scriptwriting; others offer advice on the format required for writing a screenplay. There are also computer software programs that assist with screenplay formatting.

If you want to write scripts for computer and video games, it is a good idea to play and listen to as many games as possible. Determine what makes a well-written video game successful. And on the flip side, try to pinpoint what you don't like about the script of a game that is not popular. Reading books about the field will also be useful. Two suggestions: *Game Writing: Narrative Skills for Videogames*, edited by Chris Bateman, and *Professional Techniques for Video Game Writing*, edited by Wendy Despain.

You also can create your own video game or animated short and write a script for it. This will help you learn firsthand the challenges of creating interesting characters, action, and dialogue.

EMPLOYERS

Most scriptwriters work on a freelance basis, contracting with game, film, or television production companies for individual projects. Those who work in the television industry may contract with a TV production company for a certain number of episodes or seasons. Others work for advertising agencies or educational software developers.

STARTING OUT

The first step to getting a screenplay produced is to write a letter to a producer, head designer, or hiring manager at a game company or production company describing yourself, your training, and your work. Ask if they would be interested in reading one of your scripts or viewing your demo reel if you have already contributed to a game or animated feature or short. You should also pursue a manager or agent by sending along a brief letter describing a project you're working on. A list of agents is available from the Writers Guild of America (WGA). If you receive an invitation to submit more, you'll then prepare a synopsis or treatment of the screenplay, which is usually from one to 10 pages. It should be in the form of a narrative short story, with little or no dialogue.

Whether you are a beginning or experienced screenwriter, it is best to have an agent, since studios, game companies, producers, and stars often return unsolicited manuscripts unopened to protect themselves from plagiarism charges. Agents provide access to studios and producers, interpret contracts, and negotiate deals.

It is wise to register your script ($10 for members, $20 for nonmembers) with the WGA. Although registration offers no legal protection, it is proof that on a specific date you came up with a particular idea, treatment, or script. You should also keep a detailed journal that lists the contacts you've made, the people who have read your script, etc.

ADVANCEMENT

Competition is stiff among scriptwriters, and a beginner will find it difficult to break into the field. More opportunities become available as a scriptwriter gains experience and a reputation, but that is a process that can take many years. Rejection is a common occurrence in the field of screenwriting. Most successful scriptwriters have had to submit their work to numerous game or production companies before they find one that likes their work.

Scriptwriters in the game industry can advance by being assigned to work on more prestigious games or by taking on management responsibilities for a project. Since they work so closely with game developers, many also gain enough experience to work in this career.

Once they have sold some scripts, film and television screenwriters may be able to join the WGA. Membership in the WGA guarantees the screenwriter a minimum wage for a production and other benefits such as arbitration. Some screenwriters, however, writing for minor productions, can have regular work and successful careers without WGA membership.

Those television and film screenwriters who manage to break into the business can benefit greatly from recognition in the industry. In addition to creating their own scripts, some writers are also hired to "doctor" the scripts of others, using their expertise to revise scripts for production. If a film proves very successful, a scriptwriter will be able to command higher payment, and will be able to work on high-profile productions. Some of the most talented screenwriters receive awards from the industry, most notably the Academy Award for best original or adapted screenplay.

EARNINGS

Full-time writers in the game industry with less than three years' experience earned average salaries of $51,731 in 2008, according to *Game Developer* magazine. Those with three to six years' experience averaged $59,167.

The U.S. Department of Labor reports that full-time writers employed in all fields earned salaries that ranged from less than $28,020 to more than $106,630 in 2008. It reports the following mean annual salaries for writers by industry: motion picture and video, $98,820; advertising, $71,640; television broadcasting, $63,330; and newspaper, periodical, book, and directory publishers, $51,980.

According to the WGA 2008 Theatrical and Television Basic Agreement, earnings for writers of an original screenplay ranged from $62,642 to $117,602 during the 2010–11 segment of the contract. Although these figures sound high, it is important to remember that work for scriptwriters is very cyclical. There will be times when screenwriters will be steadily busy, and others where they will be out of work for months at a time. And since many writers work as freelancers, they generally can't predict how much money they'll make from one year to the next.

Scriptwriters who are members of the WGA are eligible to receive health benefits.

WORK ENVIRONMENT

Scriptwriters who choose to freelance have the freedom to write when and where they choose. They must be persistent and patient. It is hard to break into scriptwriting in the gaming industry, and only one in 20 to 30 purchased or optioned film or television screenplays is produced.

Scriptwriters who work on the staff of a large company, for a television series, or under contract to a motion picture company or a computer game company may share writing duties with others.

Scriptwriters who do not live in cities that have a large number of game companies or film and television studios will likely have to travel to attend script conferences. They may even have to relocate for several weeks while a project is in production. Busy periods before and during film production are followed by long periods of inactivity and solitude. This forces many screenwriters, especially those just getting started in the field, to work other jobs and pursue other careers while they develop their talent and craft.

OUTLOOK

Sales in the U.S. computer and video game industry reached $9.5 billion in 2007. Computer and video games are immensely popular and recent revenue in the industry has even exceeded that of the motion picture industry. As the industry continues to grow, and game delivery platforms such as online gaming continue to expand, there will be good opportunities for scriptwriters (especially those who also work as game designers).

Employment of writers and authors in the motion picture and video industries is expected to increase faster than the average for all careers through 2016, according to the U.S. Department of Labor. Demand is increasing for well-written animated films, television shows, and commercials, which will create a need for screenwriters. Despite this prediction, there is intense competition in the television and motion picture industries for jobs. There are approximately 11,000 members of the WGA—and only a small percentage of this number specializes in writing animated films. As cable television expands and digital technology allows for more programming, new opportunities for scriptwriters may emerge. Television networks continue to need new material and new episodes for long-running animation series. Scriptwriters will continue to find opportunities with advertising agencies and educational and training video production houses, as well as on the Internet.

FOR MORE INFORMATION

This organization provides membership and career development resources to aspiring screenwriters. It offers information on careers, competitions, its annual conference, and screenplay development at its Web site.
American Screenwriters Association
269 South Beverly Drive, Suite 2600
Beverly Hills, CA 90212-3807
Tel: 866-265-9091
Email: asa@goasa.com

For information on working in the computer and video game industry, contact the following associations:
Entertainment Software Association
575 Seventh Street, NW, Suite 300
Washington, DC 20004-1611
Email: esa@theesa.com
http://www.theesa.com

International Game Developers Association
19 Mantua Road
Mt. Royal, NJ 08061-1006
Tel: 856-423-2990
http://www.igda.org

Software & Information Industry Association
1090 Vermont Avenue, NW, 6th Floor
Washington, DC 20005-4095
Tel: 202-289-7442
http://www.siia.net

This nonprofit organization is "dedicated to the advancement of the art of animation." It offers membership to anyone who is interested in animation. Visit its Web site for details on membership benefits, CARTOON magazine, screenings, volunteer opportunities, and an animation hall of fame.

The International Animated Film Society: ASIFA-Hollywood
2114 West Burbank Boulevard
Burbank, CA 91506-1232
Tel: 818-842-8330
Email: info@asifa-hollywood.org
http://www.asifa-hollywood.org

Visit the guild's Web site to learn more about the film industry, read interviews and articles by noted screenwriters, access screenwriter tools and resources, read copies of On Writing, *and find links to many other screenwriting-related sites on the Internet.*

Writers Guild of America-East Chapter
555 West 57th Street
New York, NY 10019-2925
Tel: 212-767-7800
http://www.wgaeast.org

Visit the guild's Web site to access screenwriter resources and tools, read articles such as "What Every 'Toon Writer Needs to Know," and find links to many other screenwriting- and animation-related sites on the Internet.

Writers Guild of America-West Chapter
Animation Writers Caucus
7000 West Third Street
Los Angeles, CA 90048-4329
Tel: 800-548-4532
http://www.wga.org

INTERVIEW

Corvus Elrod is a writer and storyteller and the co-owner of the Zakelro Story Studio. He also serves on the executive committee of the International Game Developers Association's Writing Special Inter-

est Group. (Visit http://www.zakelro.com to learn more about his career.) Corvus discussed his career with the editors of Careers in Focus: Animation.

Q. Why did you decide to become a game writer/story-teller?

A. I've been a storyteller and improvisational performer for all of my adult life. As I worked to make my performances more meaningful and personal to each audience member, I began to incorporate game mechanics into my skits. As I refined this process, I began to realize that the mechanics themselves—most often represented by gestures, body language, facial expression, or tone of voice—carried far more meaning than the actual words I used. I discovered that a single script, delivered as radically different characters, took on entirely new meanings when presented to an audience. This led me to begin exploring video games with a semiotics approach, that is—with an eye on how game mechanics communicate meaning. I began to see that the most powerful storytelling tools in video games were the gameplay itself and the rest of my career has unfolded from there as I explore this exciting frontier of storytelling.

Q. Can you tell us a little about the Zakelro Story Studio? Please take us through a day in your work life. What are your typical responsibilities and hours?

A. Zakelro Story Studio is a two-person studio that supports the creative projects of myself and my wife—an extraordinary storyteller in her own right. I work full time for the studio from a home office, where I am kept company by a miniature poodle we rescued named (T.S.) Eliot. I am an early riser, so I tend to put in around five hours of concentrated work before I take a couple of hours off around noon. I return to my office in the middle of the afternoon and spend another hour or two working on projects, or doing business development and networking.

I almost always work a little bit every day of the week, including weekends. This is less from necessity and more because I love what I do and if I don't spend some time working on output every day, then I start to feel mentally cluttered and I become less effective.

My time is pretty evenly divided between working on paying contracts, working on my own projects, and doing the networking that's necessary to keep the paying contracts coming in. Sometimes the latter simply involves updating my professional blog with my latest thoughts on the semiotics of game design, or following conversation threads on Twitter and Facebook. It also includes volunteer work I do for professional organizations such as the International Game Developers Association or SIGGRAPH.

Q. What do you like least and most about work as a game writer/storyteller?

A. I am hard pressed to think of anything I don't like about my career. Some days are more difficult than others. Some clients can be more challenging than others. Some projects turn out to be less fun than others. But on the whole, I am doing something that I love and I'm fortunate enough to be at a point in my life where I can be somewhat picky about the jobs I accept.

What I love most about my job is hearing from an audience about their experience with one of my games. It doesn't really even matter if the feedback is positive or negative (although it's always thrilling when it's positive), because each impression that I hear helps me express myself better next time. If you pay attention to how people receive your work, it only serves to make you better at what you do, which in turn makes it more exciting to do it.

Q. What are the most important personal and professional qualities for people in your career?

A. The three most important qualities needed for any profession are creativity, passion, and unrelenting honesty. Creativity and passion are obvious responses. The unrelenting honesty must include being honest with yourself. When something isn't working for your project, or your client, you must examine your work and improve it. When you need to "compromise" your vision to include another's ideas, you must be able to honestly assess which ideas will provide a better experience for the audience. And finally, when you create something that is really good—you must be honest enough to accept it. False modesty leads to all sorts of creative pitfalls that make a talented person's life a lot more difficult than it needs to be. This doesn't mean you need to brag, but you need to be able to honestly accept praise, just like you honestly accept criticism.

Q. What is one of the most interesting or rewarding things that has happened to you while working in the field?

A. Perhaps the most rewarding thing that has happened is when I'm contacted by a complete stranger who has either seen my work or read my blog, and has been inspired to pursue his or her own ideas about storytelling in video games. The thought that my work not only reaches audiences, but also might inspire other storytellers, is something that still sends chills down my spine.

Software Engineers

QUICK FACTS

School Subjects
Computer science
Mathematics

Personal Skills
Mechanical/manipulative
Technical/scientific

Work Environment
Primarily indoors
Primarily one location

Minimum Education Level
Bachelor's degree

Salary Range
$53,720 to $90,000 to
$150,000+

Certification or Licensing
Recommended

Outlook
Much faster than the average

DOT
030

GOE
02.07.01

NOC
2173

O*NET-SOC
15-1031.00, 15-1032.00

OVERVIEW

Software engineers create or customize existing software programs to meet the needs of a particular business or industry such as film and television studios that produce animated features or the computer and video game industry. First, they spend considerable time researching, defining, and analyzing the problem at hand. Then, they develop software programs to resolve the problem on the computer. There are approximately 857,000 computer software engineers employed in many industries in the United States.

HISTORY

The first major advances in modern computer technology were made during World War II. After the war it was thought that the enormous size of computers, which easily took up the space of entire warehouses, would limit their use to huge government projects. Accordingly, the 1950 census was computer-processed.

The introduction of semiconductors to computer technology made possible smaller and less expensive computers. Businesses began adapting computers to their operations as early as 1954. In the 1960s and beyond, technical societies, trade magazines, and computer organizations sprang up around the country as computer use became more widespread. Within 30 years computers had revolutionized the way people work, play, and go shopping. Today, computers are everywhere, from businesses of all kinds, to government agencies, charitable organizations, and private homes. Over the years, technology has continued to shrink computer size and increase speed at an unprecedented rate.

Advances in computer technology have enabled professionals to put computers to work in a range of activities once thought impossible. In the past several years computer software engineers have been able to take advantage of computer hardware improvements in speed, memory capacity, reliability, and accuracy to create programs that do just about anything. Computer engineering blossomed as a distinct subfield in the computer industry after the new performance levels were achieved. This relative lateness is explained by the fact that the programs written by software engineers to solve business and scientific problems are very intricate and complex, requiring a lot of computing power.

Animation-related industries, like many other industries, have taken advantage of the advances in computer technology. Developments in software have taken computer and video games from the primitive days of *Pong* in the 1970s to the multiplayer, multi-platform, graphically complicated games that we play today. The animated motion picture and television industries have been completely changed by the work of software engineers. Animation cels used to be laboriously drawn and colored by hand and filmed using conventional motion picture cameras. Today, advances in computer software and hardware allow animators to create their work directly on the computer—eliminating time-consuming and costly steps in the production process.

Although many computer scientists will continue to focus their research on further developing hardware, the emphasis in the field has moved more squarely to software, and it is predicted that software engineers will be one of the fastest growing occupations in the United States through the next decade. Given this, software engineering will play a significant role in animation-related industries for years to come.

THE JOB

Computer software engineers define and analyze specific problems and help develop computer software applications that effectively solve them. Software engineers fall into two basic categories: *systems software engineers,* who build and maintain entire computer systems for a company; and *applications software engineers,* who design, create, and modify general computer applications software or specialized utility programs. Additionally, within the computer and video game industry, for example, software engineers can either work on the computer systems and software applications of a computer and video game company, such as a game development studio, computer and video game publisher, or manufacturer of computer and video game platforms; or they can work directly on computer and video game product development—for example, writing code for a video game or assisting in the programming of a video game console.

Systems software engineers who work on computer systems research how a company's departments and their respective computer systems are organized. They suggest ways to coordinate all these parts. They might set up intranets or networks that link computers within the organization and ease communication.

Some applications software engineers develop packaged software applications, such as word processing, graphic design, or database programs for software development companies. Other applications software engineers design customized software or tools for individual businesses or organizations. For example, an applications software engineer might work with a video console manufacturer to develop new ways to reduce paperwork in the areas of sales and orders, returns, and bill processing. An engineer who is employed by DreamWorks Animation SKG might be tasked with developing new proprietary character animation tools or maintaining existing tools. An engineer at Pixar may be responsible for developing proprietary 3D filmmaking software that will be used to create feature films. Applications software engineers write programs using programming languages like C++ and Java. Engineers have created software programs such as Maya, Final Cut, Premiere, and After Effects that help animators do their jobs more effectively. (One program, Macromedia's Flash, has given rise to an entire Internet cartoon subculture.)

Both systems and applications software engineering involve extremely detail-oriented work. Since computers do only what they are programmed to do, engineers have to account for every bit of information with a programming command. Software engineers are thus required to be very well organized and precise. In order to achieve this, they generally follow strict procedures in completing an assignment.

First, they interview clients and colleagues in order to determine exactly what they want the final program to accomplish. Defining the problem by outlining the goal can sometimes be difficult. Then, engineers evaluate the software applications already in use by the client to understand how and why they are failing to fulfill the needs of the operation. After this period of fact gathering, the engineers use methods of scientific analysis and mathematical models to develop possible solutions to the problems. These analytical

A software engineer at a video game developer sits at her multi-screen workstation. *(Lenny Ignelzi, AP Photo)*

methods help them predict and measure the outcomes of different proposed designs.

When they have developed a clear idea of what type of program is required to fulfill the client's needs, they draw up a detailed proposal that includes estimates of time and cost allocations. Management must then decide if the project will meet their needs, is a good investment, and whether or not it will be undertaken.

Once a proposal is accepted, both software engineers and technicians begin work on the project. They verify with hardware engineers that the proposed software program can be completed with existing hardware systems. Typically, the engineer writes program specifications and the technician uses his or her knowledge of computer languages to write preliminary programming. Engineers focus most of their effort on program strategies, testing procedures, and reviewing technicians' work.

Software engineers are usually responsible for a significant amount of technical writing, including project proposals, progress reports, and user manuals. They are required to meet regularly with clients in order to keep project goals clear and learn about any changes as quickly as possible.

When the program is completed, the software engineer organizes a demonstration of the final product to the client. Supervisors, management, and users are generally present. Some software engineers may offer to install the program, train users on it, and make arrangements for ongoing technical support.

Software engineers working directly with computer and video games often have very similar job duties to those of a computer programmer working in the same field. However, there are some differences between the two positions. Software engineers have formal training in methods of scientific analysis. In general, programmers are concerned with writing code for a game, whereas engineers are concerned with not just writing the code, but how that code relates to the game application in which it will be used, or how that code figures in the "big picture" in terms of what is to be accomplished. Software engineers can be game programmers, but not all game programmers have the skills to be software engineers. Regardless, in many computer and video game companies there is a lot of overlap between the two positions and the terms are often used interchangeably.

Software engineering technicians sometimes assist software engineers in completing projects. They are usually knowledgeable in analog, digital, and microprocessor electronics and programming techniques. Technicians know enough about program design and computer languages to fill in details left out by engineers, who conceive of the program from a large-scale perspective. Technicians might also test new software applications with special diagnostic equipment.

REQUIREMENTS

High School

If you are interested in pursuing this career, take as many computer, math, and science courses as possible, because they provide fundamental math and computer knowledge and teach analytical thinking skills. Classes that rely on schematic drawing and flowcharts are also very valuable. English and speech courses will help you improve your communication skills, which are very important for software engineers.

Postsecondary Training

In the past, the computer industry has tended to be fairly flexible about official credentials; demonstrated computer proficiency and work experience have often been enough to obtain a good position.

As more and more well-educated professionals enter the industry, however, it is becoming more important for you to have at least a bachelor's degree in computer science, software engineering, or programming.

Certification or Licensing
Many software engineers pursue commercial certification. These programs are usually run by computer companies that wish to train professionals to work with their products. Classes are challenging and examinations can be rigorous. New programs are introduced every year. In addition, professional certification as a certified software development professional is now offered by the Institute of Electrical and Electronics Engineers (IEEE) Computer Society. The Institute for Certification of Computing Professionals also offers general certifications to computer professionals.

Other Requirements
As a software engineer, you will need strong communication skills in order to be able to make formal business presentations and interact with people having different levels of computer expertise. You must also be detail oriented. Working with programming languages and intense details is often frustrating. Therefore, you should be patient, enjoy problem-solving challenges, and work well under pressure. If you plan to work in an animation-related field, it is a good idea to have at least some familiarity with your chosen specialty (such as computer and video games).

EXPLORING
In general, you should be intent on learning as much as possible about computers, computer software, and animation-related technology. You should learn about new developments by reading trade magazines and talking to other computer users. You also can join computer clubs and surf the Internet for information about working in this field. Visit the Web site of the International Game Developers Association (http://archives.igda.org/breakingin) to check out "Breaking In: Preparing for Your Career in Games." This free online resource offers an overview of the different jobs—including engineers—available in the game industry and features job profiles and interviews with workers in the field.

Try to spend a day with a working software engineer or technician in order to experience firsthand what the job is like. School guidance counselors can help you arrange such a visit. You can also talk to your high school computer teacher for more information.

High school and college students who have computer skills may be able to obtain part-time jobs or internships at animation studios or game companies. Any computer experience will be helpful for future computer training.

EMPLOYERS

Approximately 857,000 computer software engineers are employed in many areas of business in the United States. Approximately 507,000 work with applications and 350,000 work with systems software. In the computer and video game industry, most software engineers are employed by the manufacturers of the various computer and video game platforms, computer and video game publishers, and game development studios. These companies are usually located in major cities, especially on the East and West Coasts. A significant number of game companies are also located in Illinois and Texas. Major entertainment software publishers include Electronic Arts, Nintendo of America, Atari, Sony, Activision Blizzard, THQ, Take-Two Interactive, Microsoft, and Konami Digital Entertainment-America.

Software engineers are also employed by television and film animation studios (such as Pixar, Walt Disney Animation Studios, Blue Sky Studios, Rhythm & Hues Studios, and DreamWorks Animation SKG), large advertising agencies that specialize in animation, and independent animators.

Outside of animation-related industries, software engineering is done in many fields, including medical, industrial, military, communications, aerospace, scientific, and other commercial businesses. The majority of software engineers, though, are employed by computer and data processing companies and by consulting firms.

STARTING OUT

As a college student, you should work closely with your school's career services office given that many professionals find their first position through on-campus recruiting. Career services office staff are well trained to provide tips on resume writing, interviewing techniques, and locating job leads.

Individuals not working with a school career services office can check the classified ads for job openings. Software engineers who are specifically interested in working in animation-related industries should visit the following Web sites for job leads: Animation World Network (http://www.awn.com), HighendCareers (http://www.highendcareers.com), Dice (http://www.dice.com), GameJobs (http://www.gamejobs.com), and Gamasutra (http://www.gamasutra.com).

Some software engineers interested in the game industry attend trade shows (such as the annual Computer Game Developers Conference) where they can meet recruiters looking for people to work at their companies. Information on the conference is available at http://www.gdconf.com.

ADVANCEMENT

Software engineers who demonstrate leadership qualities and thorough technical know-how may become *project team leaders* who are responsible for full-scale game software development projects. Project team leaders oversee the work of technicians and other engineers. They determine the overall parameters of a project, calculate time schedules and financial budgets, divide the project into smaller tasks, and assign these tasks to engineers. Overall, they do both managerial and technical work.

Software engineers with experience as project team leaders may be promoted to a position as *software manager,* running a large research and development department. Managers oversee software projects with a more encompassing perspective; they help choose projects to be undertaken, select project team leaders and engineering teams, and assign individual projects. In some cases they may be required to travel, solicit new business, and contribute to the general marketing strategy of the company.

Many computer professionals find that their interests change over time. As long as individuals are well qualified and keep up to date with the latest technology, they are usually able to find positions in other areas of the computer industry.

EARNINGS

Software engineers with a bachelor's degree in computer engineering earned starting salaries of $56,201 in 2007, according to the National Association of Colleges and Employers. Computer engineers in all fields who specialized in applications earned median annual salaries of $85,430 in 2008, according to the U.S.

Department of Labor. The lowest paid 10 percent averaged less than $53,720, and the highest paid 10 percent earned $128,870 or more annually. Software engineers in all fields who specialized in systems software earned median salaries of $92,430 in 2008. The lowest paid 10 percent averaged $57,810 annually, and the highest paid engineers made $135,780 per year. Experienced software engineers can earn more than $150,000 a year. When software engineers are promoted to project team leader or software manager, they earn even more.

Most software engineers work for companies that offer extensive benefits, including health insurance, sick leave, and paid vacation. In some smaller game companies, however, benefits may be limited.

WORK ENVIRONMENT

Software engineers usually work in comfortable office environments. Overall, they usually work 40-hour weeks, but this depends on the nature of the employer and expertise of the engineer. In animation-related industries, long work hours are typical. In consulting firms, for example, it is typical for engineers to work long hours and frequently travel to out-of-town assignments.

Software engineers generally receive an assignment and a time frame within which to accomplish it; daily work details are often left up to the individuals. Some engineers work relatively lightly at the beginning of a project, but work a lot of overtime at the end in order to catch up. Most engineers are not compensated for overtime. Software engineering can be stressful, especially when engineers must work to meet deadlines.

OUTLOOK

The field of software engineering is expected to be one of the fastest growing occupations through 2016, according to the U.S. Department of Labor. Demands made on computers increase every day and from all industries, including the game and film and television industries. The development of one kind of software sparks ideas for many others. In addition, users rely on software programs that are increasingly user-friendly.

Since technology changes so rapidly, software engineers are advised to keep up on the latest developments. While the need for software engineers will remain high, computer languages will probably change every few years and software engineers will need to attend seminars and workshops to learn new computer languages and software design. They also should read trade magazines (especially those that relate to their particular industry), surf the Internet, and talk with colleagues about the field. These kinds of continuing education techniques help ensure that software engineers are best equipped to meet the needs of the workplace.

FOR MORE INFORMATION

For industry information, contact the following organizations:
Association for Computing Machinery
Two Penn Plaza, Suite 701
New York, NY 10121-0701
Tel: 800-342-6626
http://www.acm.org

Entertainment Software Association
575 Seventh Street, NW, Suite 300
Washington, DC 20004-1611
Email: esa@theesa.com
http://www.theesa.com

For information on careers and education, student memberships, and to read Careers in Computer Science and Computer Engineering, *contact*
IEEE Computer Society
2001 L Street NW, Suite 700
Washington, DC 20036-4910
Tel: 202-371-0101
Email: help@computer.org
http://www.computer.org

For information on careers in the game industry, contact
International Game Developers Association
19 Mantua Road
Mt. Royal, NJ 08061-1006
Tel: 856-423-2990
http://www.igda.org

For certification information, contact
Institute for Certification of Computing Professionals
2400 East Devon Avenue, Suite 281
Des Plaines, IL 60018-4629

Tel: 800-843-8227
http://www.iccp.org

For more information on careers in computer software, contact
Software and Information Industry Association
1090 Vermont Avenue, NW, 6th Floor
Washington, DC 20005-4095
Tel: 202-289-7442
http://www.siia.net

Sound Workers

OVERVIEW

Sound workers create the audio aspects of computer and video games, animated features and shorts, animations in commercials, and other animated products (such as training simulations used by the military).

HISTORY

Although the first animated cartoon was created in 1892, it was not until the mid-1920s that technological innovations allowed sound to be added effectively to cartoons. One example of the effect that sound had on animated films can be illustrated by the story of the Mickey Mouse cartoons, as detailed in *Animation Art: From Pencil to Pixel, The History of Cartoon, Anime, and CGI*. Walt Disney, the founder of the Disney entertainment empire, created the Mickey Mouse character in the late 1920s. Sound was not used for the first two cartoon shorts that featured the now world-famous mouse, and the cartoons were not popular. Disney decided that the third Mickey Mouse short, *Steamboat Willie* (1928), would be made using "synchronized sounds and music." He hired Carl Edouarde and his band to record the music for *Steamboat Willie* while watching a copy of the short. Pat Powers, an early audio professional, then matched the music with the animation reel to create a final product. This combination of sound, animation, and a likable "star" helped the Mickey Mouse cartoons become a hit—and brought Walt Disney fame and fortune. Music, sound effects, and voice tracks quickly became key components of animated shorts and feature films. Today, it is hard to imagine an animated film or commercial without sound. Dialogue, sound effects, and music play a major role in the mood, tone, and plot of animated movies and shorts, and there are many different types of sound professionals who help create audio magic.

The computer and video game industry did not begin to develop until the 1960s and 1970s. At the beginning of the video game age, developers naturally focused on game play and visuals. Today, with ever-faster computer processors, increasing storage space, a variety of equipment on which to play—from the Internet to the home console—and sophisticated recording and editing software and hardware, sound workers are gaining in both importance and the respect they receive. Audio is one of the most rapidly developing areas of game work, and many in the industry see this field as one that will have dynamic future growth.

THE JOB

Some sound workers are employed by large, well-known companies, such as Nintendo or Pixar, on a full-time basis. Many sound workers, however, work on a contract basis, meaning that they are freelancers who are hired by companies to work on a particular project, and sometimes a particular aspect of a particular project, until it is completed. Because of this and other factors, such as the size of the employer, sound workers are referred to by a number of job titles. In addition, they may be responsible for many types of sound production or focus on only a few sound areas.

Sound designers are responsible for all of the sound used in a computer or video game, animated film, or commercial. They create the squealing noise of a race car's tires, the squish of a character walking through mud, the zap from an alien's weapon, or the crunching thud of one football player tackling another. They are also responsible for any talking, singing, yelling, and so on, that characters in the game, film, or commercial do. Finally, they create or find recordings of all of the music to be used in the film or game. All the sounds must fit in with its action and setting in order to catch the interest of the intended audience and increase their emotional experience. Therefore, to do their job successfully, sound workers must work well with other team members to ensure that the sound they create fits just right.

To understand the work of a sound designer, here is an example of the responsibilities of a sound designer employed in the computer and video game industry. The first team members that sound designers usually consult are the game designers. It is the sound designer's job to find out what look and feel the game designers want. To do this, the sound designer may look at concept sketches and ask the game designers questions. How many levels of play will there be? Who is the intended audience? Where will the game be played (for example, in an arcade, on the Internet, or on a home console)? Does the game take place in a particular time period, such as 100 years in the future or during the Civil War? Answers to questions like these give sound designers a framework for their work. For example, if the game will be played in an arcade, the designer will know to make sounds louder and simpler than for a game played on a console at home. If the game takes place in the past, for example, the sound designer may need to do research to find out what musical instruments were used at that time and then find ways to reproduce their sound.

Sound designers also frequently work with artists and animators. To enhance the game, sound designers must make sure the characters' voices somehow complement their looks as well as match up with the artists and animators' visions of their personalities. For example, the sound designer needs to know if a large, bear-like character should have a deep, slow-speaking, friendly voice or a squeaky, fast-speaking, unpleasant voice. Voices also need to match up with the character's actions. In some sports games, for example, a commentator may speak during much of the game but will need to adjust his or her voice—from fast and excited to disappointed to surprised, and so on—to suit the events. Sound designers also work with game programmers to ensure that the final sound produced is what was desired. Although sound designers generally don't have to write the programming code, those who have coding knowledge are at an advantage because they have a good understanding of both the programmer's job and how to achieve the best sound style.

Sound designers employed in any animation-related industry usually have access to a "sound library," recordings of many different sounds. But they must also know how to create and record their own sounds for use in a product. This can mean recording sounds that will be used realistically in a game or animated feature; for example, recording the noise of a passing train to use in a scene with a passing train. It can also mean recording sounds to go with imaginary action; for example, recording a rotten apple hitting a brick wall to use for the sound of a zombie being punched in the stomach. Sound designers create music using special software and equipment, such as a keyboard that simulates many instruments. They may write the music, play it, and record it (or they may hire *composers* and *musicians* to write and perform the music). Occasionally they may make a recording of live music and even be responsible for finding the right musicians for the work. In addition, game designers and animation directors sometimes ask the sound designer to use music that has already been produced, such as songs from a popular band. For example, *Tony Hawk's Pro Skater* incorporates music from well-known punk rock bands such as Motorhead and the Ramones. The popular animated feature film *Shrek* featured music from Smash Mouth and The Proclaimers. *Music licensors* are the professionals who negotiate with music labels and up-and-coming bands for the rights to use music in games, commercials, and animated films and television shows. In that case, either the sound designer or a music licensor needs to get permission to use the music from the recording label. Sound designers also record the *actors* who do the voice-overs for the game characters. Again, sound designers are sometimes responsible for finding actors to do this work, or they may do some of the voice-overs themselves.

The extent of sound designers' responsibilities depends a great deal on factors such as their experience, the size of the employer, and the budget for creating the product. In an environment that offers the opportunity to specialize, such as at a large company, there may be sound designers who work only on sound effects. These *sound effects designers* concentrate on creating the noises for specific events in a game, animated feature, or commercial—a car crash, a baseball being hit, a bomb exploding, and so on—as well as background noises, such as rain falling or a dog barking far away.

Composers are sound specialists who focus on creating the music for a game, animated feature, or commercial. They need to be able to write music in many different styles—techno, rock, and even classical—for different products and to create many different moods. Frequently composers know how to play an instrument on their own, and many find that knowing how to play the piano, synthesizers, or samplers is particularly helpful. Some composers in the animation industry are well known. For example, the singer/songwriter Randy Newman wrote the music for the animation smash hit *Toy Story*. Musicians perform, compose, conduct, and arrange music. They may work alone or as part of a group to create music. Some composers and musicians may also have additional duties as sound designers or sound effects designers. To create the various types of sound and music that appear in animated creations, composers and musicians may work from storyboards; a finished game, animated feature, or commercial; or nothing but an idea or concept for the product.

Sound directors are responsible for managing sound workers such as musicians, singers, *audio recording engineers* (who oversee the technical end of sound recordings), sound designers, and *recording*

Actress Janeane Garofalo, the voice of Collette in *Ratatouille*, prepares to read her lines during a voice recording session. *(Pixar-Disney/Topham/The Image Works)*

mixers (who combine music and sound effects with an animated film or video game's action).

REQUIREMENTS

High School

If you are interested in becoming a sound worker, you should take computer science and math, including algebra and geometry. You should also take history, English, and other college prep classes. Of course, take as many music classes as possible and learn how to play one or more musical instruments, especially the piano, synthesizer, and keyboard.

Postsecondary Training

In the past most sound designers learned their trade through on-the-job training. Today, many sound designers are earning bachelor's degrees in music, sound design, or audio engineering, and this will probably become more necessary as technologies become more complex. Typical programs focus on computer and music studies, including music history, music theory, composition, sound design, and audio engineering.

If you are interested in becoming a composer or musician, you can continue your education in any of numerous colleges and universities or special music schools or conservatories that offer bachelor's and higher degrees. Your course of study will include music history, music criticism, music theory, harmony, counterpoint, rhythm, melody, and ear training. In most major music schools, courses in composition are offered along with orchestration and arranging. Courses are also taught covering voice and the major musical instruments, including keyboard, guitar, and, more recently, synthesizer. Most schools now cover computer techniques as applied to music as well. Audio recording engineers and mixers can prepare for the field by taking seminars and workshops and by pursuing degrees in music engineering and technology at technical schools or community colleges.

Other Requirements

Sound designers need to be able to use the latest technologies to record, edit, and "sweeten" their work. Workers in this field are continuously updating their skills, learning how to use new tools or techniques to create the sounds they want. Composers and musicians need to have a passion for music; an interest in computer and video games, animated features, or commercials; and a high degree of dedication, self-discipline, and drive. All sound workers should also have strong communication skills to be able to work with a diverse group of industry professionals and have flexibility to work with a variety of musical genres.

EXPLORING

If you are interested in becoming a sound worker, you can start experimenting with sounds and effects on your computer at home. Listen to current games or animated films and try to re-create their sounds or work with a group of friends to create a brand new game or film that contains sound effects and music that you have come up with on your own.

The Internet is a great place to learn more about the computer and video game industry and sound careers. Online publications such as *Game Developer* (http://www.gdmag.com) will provide you with an overview of opportunities in the industry. You can also visit *Music4Games* (http://www.music4games.net) to read reviews of current games and production tools, as well as interviews with those in the field. Check out http://www.audiogang.org, the site for the Game Audio Network Guild, which offers student membership. You also might want to read the online resource, "Breaking In: Preparing For Your Career in Games," which is available at the International Game Developers Association's Web site (http://archives.

igda.org/breakingin). It offers an overview of sound careers, profiles of workers in the field, and other resources. Another way to learn more about the field is to attend the annual Game Developers Conference. This will allow you to meet people in the business and other enthusiasts, see new games and technologies, and even attend workshops of interest to you. Of course, this event can be expensive, but if your funds are limited, you may want to work as a student volunteer, which enables you to pay much less. Visit http://www.gdconf.com for more information about this conference.

If you are interested in working as a sound worker in the film and television industries, you should listen to the soundtracks and music of as many animated films, shorts, and commercials that you can. You can also try to participate in an information interview with sound workers in these fields and visit Web sites that offer more information. You can read profiles of well-known composers and other sound workers at the Internet Movie Database (http://us.imdb.com) and find links to the Web sites of prominent composers and songwriters by visiting The Film Music Society's Web site (http://www.filmmusicsociety.org).

EMPLOYERS

Sound workers are employed by computer game companies and developers, film and television animation studios, and advertising agencies. Some sound professionals, especially composers and musicians, work on a freelance or project basis. Many positions in animation-related industries are located on the East and West Coasts (namely California and New York City) and aspiring sound workers may have to relocate to these regions to find work in the industry.

Other opportunities for sound workers are found in the recording, music video, and radio industries. Composers can try to sell their work to music publishers, recording companies, dance companies, and musical theater producers. Musicians can work for religious organizations, orchestras, schools, clubs, restaurants, and cruise lines; at weddings; and in opera and ballet productions.

STARTING OUT

Sound workers can learn more about jobs in the computer and video game industry by visiting game company Web sites and sites that advertise job openings, such as GameJobs (http://www.gamejobs.com) and Gamasutra (http://www.gamasutra.com). Many people attend the annual Game Developers Conference to network and learn more about internship and job opportunities. Other industry Web sites such as HighendCareers (http://www.highendcareers.com) and Dice (http://www.dice.com) offer information on jobs and employers.

Sound workers who want to work in the motion picture or television industries should contact animation companies such as Pixar, Walt Disney Animation Studios, and DreamWorks Animation SKG directly. They can also find job listings at AnimationWorldNetwork (http://www.awn.com). Those who want to create sound for commercials and other advertising should contact advertising agencies directly for more information on employment opportunities.

Aspiring composers and musicians usually break into the industry by creating a demo tape of their work and submitting it along with a resume to game companies. They might also create a Web site that features samples of their work for potential employers to review.

ADVANCEMENT

With experience, sound workers at software publishers can advance to the position of *music* or *audio director* and oversee the work of sound designers and other professionals. Others might start their own companies and provide services to game companies or animation studios on a freelance basis. Advancement for composers and musicians often takes place on a highly personal level. As they become known for their artistic abilities, they may be asked to compose or perform music for more prestigious projects or companies. Some may become well-known composers and musicians in the film and television industries or in the fine arts.

EARNINGS

Game Developer magazine reports that sound designers in the computer and video game industry earned approximately $78,167 in 2008. Those employed by software publishers earned $61,620, and those who worked in the advertising industry earned $68,470 a year. Composers/arrangers with three to six years' experience earned average annual salaries of $80,192. According to the International Game Developers Association, salaries for sound workers range from $45,000 to $130,000, with an average of $57,500 annually.

Sound engineering technicians employed in the motion picture and video industries earned mean annual salaries of $60,600 in 2008, according to the U.S. Department of Labor. Musicians employed in the motion picture and video industries earned mean hourly wages of $37.70 in 2008.

The American Federation of Musicians of the United States and Canada has created pay scales for musicians and composers who perform or write music for computer and video games and for motion picture and television films (including animated features). Contact the federation for the latest rates.

Full-time sound workers receive typical fringe benefits such as paid vacation and sick days, health insurance, and the opportunity to participate in retirement savings plans. Freelance sound workers must pay for their own health insurance and other benefits.

WORK ENVIRONMENT

Sound designers work in recording studios that are usually air conditioned because of the sensitivity of the equipment. Studios may be loud or cramped, however, especially during recording sessions where many people are working in a small space. Some designers may be required to record off-site, at live concerts, for example, or other places where the recording is to take place.

The physical conditions of a composer's workplace can vary according to personal taste and what is affordable. Some work in expensive, state-of-the-art home studios, others in a bare room with an electric keyboard or a guitar. Musicians on animation-related projects may work in recording studios, home studios, or at concert halls and other venues.

OUTLOOK

Although the use of sound in computer and video games, animated features and shorts, and commercials is growing in importance, sound workers still make up a very small portion of professionals in these industries. As a result, competition for jobs is very strong. Sound workers who have a combined knowledge of sound design and composition and/or musical abilities will have good employment prospects over the next decade. The rarest breed of sound worker in the computer and video game industry is the professional who has expertise in both sound and game programming. Demand for these specialized workers will be especially strong over the next decade. Likewise, sound workers with knowledge of filmmaking techniques will have better employment prospects than workers with only a background in music.

FOR MORE INFORMATION

For information on union pay scales for musicians employed in the game or film and television industries, contact
American Federation of Musicians of the United States and Canada
1501 Broadway, Suite 600
New York, NY 10036-5501

Tel: 212-869-1330
http://www.afm.org

For information on student membership and audio recording schools and courses, contact
Audio Engineering Society
60 East 42nd Street, Room 2520
New York, NY 10165-2520
Tel: 212-661-8528
http://www.aes.org

For industry information, contact
Entertainment Software Association
575 Seventh Street, NW, Suite 300
Washington, DC 20004-1611
Email: esa@theesa.com
http://www.theesa.com

This organization "promotes the preservation of film and television music." Visit its Web site for more information.
The Film Music Society
1516 South Bundy Drive, Suite 305
Los Angeles, CA 90025-2683
Tel: 310-820-1909
Email: info@filmmusicsociety.org
http://www.filmmusicsociety.org

For information on membership and industry awards for sound workers, contact
Game Audio Network Guild
1611-A South Melrose Drive, #290
Vista, CA 92081-5471
http://www.audiogang.org

For general information on the game industry, visit
Game Developer Magazine
http://www.gdmag.com

For comprehensive career information, including "Breaking In: Preparing For Your Career in Games," visit the association's Web site.
International Game Developers Association
19 Mantua Road
Mt. Royal, NJ 08061-1006

Tel: 856-423-2990
http://www.igda.org

For information on music careers, contact
MENC: The National Association for Music Education
1806 Robert Fulton Drive
Reston, VA 20191-4348
Tel: 800-336-3768
http://www.menc.org

To read interviews with sound workers and listen to music from popular video games, visit
Music4Games
http://www.music4games.net

NASM is an organization of schools, colleges, and universities that provide music education. Visit its Web site for a listing of NASM-accredited institutions.
National Association of Schools of Music (NASM)
11250 Roger Bacon Drive, Suite 21
Reston, VA 20190-5248
Tel: 703-437-0700
Email: info@arts-accredit.org
http://nasm.arts-accredit.org

This is a membership organization for "professional film/TV/multimedia music composers, songwriters, and lyricists." Visit its Web site for career resources, an online hall of fame, information on membership for college students, and The SCORE, *its quarterly publication.*
Society of Composers & Lyricists
8447 Wilshire Boulevard, Suite 401
Beverly Hills CA 90211-3209
Tel: 310-281-2812
http://www.thescl.com/site/scl

For information on membership, contact
Society of Professional Audio Recording Services
PO Box 822643
Dallas, TX 75382-2643
Tel: 800-771-7727
Email: info@spars.com
http://www.spars.com

Supporting Artists

QUICK FACTS

School Subjects
Art
Computer science
Mathematics

Personal Skills
Artistic
Communication/ideas

Work Environment
Primarily indoors
Primarily one location

Minimum Education Level
Some postsecondary training

Salary Range
$31,570 to $71,910 to
$100,390+

Certification or Licensing
None available

Outlook
About as fast as the average

DOT
N/A

GOE
N/A

NOC
5241

O*NET-SOC
27-1014.00

OVERVIEW

Supporting artists are responsible for creating all characters and backgrounds of an animation project. They create visual drawings and two- and three-dimensional forms using different media, including paints, pencil, clay, or various computer software programs. Artists work with other animation professionals, depending on their assignment, including writers, directors, animators, and producers, to get the proper style of a character or background setting, or to capture the vision of the project.

HISTORY

Supporting artists have been in demand ever since the early days of animation. But their duties and required skill sets have increased as animated films have become more technologically complex. Today, supporting artists use a combination of traditional tools and materials and knowledge of computer software design programs to help make animated films, shorts, television shows, and animated music videos and commercials seem realistic and visually pleasing.

THE JOB

In addition to directors, producers, and animators, it takes a variety of support workers to create award-winning animated features and shorts. To create *Toy Story*, for example, it took a team of talented supporting artists to take a simple concept or sketch of the cowboy doll, Woody, and transform it into a complete animated character—one with vivid colors, a distinct style, a unique personality who lived in an identifiable environment. The following paragraphs detail some of the key artists involved in creating works of animation.

Stylists work with writers and animation directors during a project's preproduction stage. Besides a script, an illustrated story line must be presented to studio or industry heads in order to attract interest and financing for a project. Stylists design the look of characters, both principal and secondary characters. They often use different media for their drawings, including color pencils, pastels, or acrylics. Some stylists may choose to use different computer software programs in addition to hand drawings. Often, stylists may need to work with writers or directors to develop the character's different qualities—facial expressions, clothing, and coloring—until the desired effects are attained.

Animated features begin as an original story idea or they are adapted from a treasured work of literature or other art form. *Visual development artists,* along with other members of a creative team, work with different aspects of the story idea, including character and plot line, color and texture scheme, background settings, and lighting or prop design. They work closely with production designers and art directors to maintain a certain mood, whether the feature is a drama or comedy.

Before production can begin, writers and the director consult with *storyboard artists* to help create a plan for the film. As with many animated or action films, storyboard artists may be given loosely sketched drawings along with a description of what certain action scenes or characters should look like, as well as the director's vision of the movie. They take this information and create their interpretation of the story in a storyboard format—individual drawings of key action sequences, along with dialogue and written instruction for layout and design. Storyboard artists may go through many drafts before their work matches the director's vision. Some storyboard artists still create these boards by hand, while many choose to use software programs such as StoryBoard Quick, Poser, or FrameForge 3D Studio. Regardless of the media they use, storyboard artists must have an eye for perspective and an understanding of camera angles. Depending on the project, storyboard artists may need to conduct research on many different topics, including history, costumes, landscapes, or architecture. Some storyboard artists may work as freelancers, though larger studios and digital effects companies such as Pixar or Digital Domain may employ a staff of storyboard artists.

Layout artists arrange a rough organizational layout of the animated feature, short, or commercial. They refer to storyboards and work closely with editors to create a suggested flow for the animation—for example, placing characters in certain spots or using rough effects to indicate where an explosion or fight might take place.

These layouts aren't part of the finished product. Instead, they serve as guide or stage for the animation team and other departments to do their work.

Modelers use storyboard sketches and the writer's script to create a 3D version of a character, animal, or even background scenery or special effects; these objects and backgrounds are integral to the development of a cartoon or movie. Modelers may use different approaches depending upon the task or their specialty. Some modelers build their geometric models using materials such as clay, latex, or wire mesh. Many animated features today are created using computer-generated imagery. Modelers using this technique create their 3D models using graphics software programs such as Maya, form•Z, bonzai, 3ds Max, Softimage, LightWave, or Blender. The process is similar to that detailed earlier, though instead of molding and sculpting 3D characters out of a physical material, modelers create geometric structures on their computer screens.

Riggers create a digital 3D skeletal structure that is used to manipulate computer-generated characters. This structure establishes how characters can bend and move.

After animators draw key frames—important motion movements within a series of frames—artists known as *inbetweeners* are responsible for drawing the remaining frames in between key frames. Key frames and inbetween frames are tied together to create the action of an animated feature. Inbetweeners are supervised by animators or animator assistants. This entry-level position is a great way to break into the animation industry.

When a film's schedule or operating budget cannot accommodate the costly setup of complicated sets, directors often turn to the talents of *matte painters*. Matte painters create foreground, midground, and background scenes for films and animated features and shorts, such as cityscapes, desert scenes, or famous landmarks using paints or pastels. Much of their work is currently done on a computer using 3D tools (such as Cinema 4D) and various software programs (such as Adobe Photoshop). A recent example of their work can be seen in the final scene of the movie, *Raiders of the Lost Ark*. The gigantic government warehouse stacked high with wooden crates was actually painted on glass by a painter; the actor's live action was filmed against a green screen and later integrated with the painted background. Matte paintings that were created using computer technology have figured prominently in films such as *The Chronicles of Riddick, Superman Returns,* and those in *The Lord of the Rings* series.

What would the character SpongeBob SquarePants be without the talents of *background artists*? This yellow sponge and his pals could be living in a nondescript small town anywhere in the world. Thanks to background artists, however, SpongeBob SquarePants is right where he should be—in the deep ocean metropolitan city known as Bikini Bottom, complete with pineapple houses, boat highways, and jellyfish parks. Background artists work with writers and layout artists to determine how the background should appear in an animated film or short. Is there a particular color scheme, mood, or other details to consider? They may use a variety of media such as watercolor, acrylics, pastels, or bits of other materials or embellishments. The background—consisting of city or landscape, key buildings, or other details—are painted on separate cels which are later layered over with character painted cels. Software programs such as Corel Painter, Adobe Illustrator, and Photoshop have allowed background artists to create much of their work on computers, which is later composited with characters or action sequences.

When an animated feature calls for the lead character to be a brown dog, for example, it is the *3D texture painter* who gets to decide (in consultation with the director) what shade of brown, and if the dog's coat will be flat and smooth, or long and shaggy. Texture painters have the important job of deciding what shades of colors and textures will look best, and work with the overall personality of the character. They work to create the proper color scheme and attributes for all characters, as well as any background environments. Texture painters may work with traditional mediums, but may use computer programs, at times writing their own programs to create unique colors or textures.

Inkers outline an artist's drawing of a character on a celluloid sheet using black ink (traditional animation) or onto a computer screen by using digital software programs (computer-generated animation). *Painters* then fill in the outlines using a series of numbered colors. A standard palette of colors is used to ensure uniformity. Software programs have revolutionized this step, with much of inking and painting work now done on computer.

Production artists work for the project's designers to create a computer layout of graphics, audio, video, charts and graphs, or storyboards. They may also be responsible for compiling, tagging, and filing final files or clips to be later transferred onto to film. Production artists may also be called upon for support on HTML editing, document tracking, or database management for a project. On larger projects, production artists may oversee several assistant production artists to help manage the workflow.

Digital effects artists are often called upon to create postproduction effects for feature films, especially when real life effects would prove too costly, dangerous, or simply impossible. For example, a

A storyboard artist creates the storyboard for a children's cartoon called *Higglytown Heroes*. *(Jakub Mosur, AP Photo)*

crucial scene in the movie *Titanic* had the survivors floating in the waters of the Atlantic, watching as the doomed ocean liner slowly sank into the ocean. Producers did not have to go through the expense of re-creating the sinking of the *Titanic* with a real ship, but rather had a team of talented digital effects artists create this moment complete with details such as breaking metal, fires, and ocean waves. Digital effects artists confer with other members of the visual department, directors, and producers to create the needed effects or backgrounds on computer. Their work is then composited with live action sequences or computer-animated sequences to create important scenes in a movie.

REQUIREMENTS
High School
Art (including drawing), graphic design, computer science, and animation classes will help you prepare for the field. Many supporting artists have college degrees, so you should take a college preparatory curriculum in high school.

Postsecondary Training
Supporting artists often have associate's or bachelor's degrees in design, animation, illustration, or related fields. Others train for the field by receiving on-the-job training. The Animation World Net-

work offers a database of animation schools at its Web site (http://schools.awn.com). Another good source of schools can be found at the International Game Developers Association's Web site (http://archives.igda.org/bre akingin/resource_schools.php).

Other Requirements

Personal and professional skills for supporting artists vary by position. Storyboard artists, for example, should have good drawing, storytelling, and staging and composition skills. Background artists need strong observational skills, a comprehensive knowledge of color and lighting, and an understanding of the animation process.

All supporting artists should be artistically talented, creative, well organized, have strong communication skills, and be willing to continue to learn throughout their careers. They also need to be able to follow instructions and be able to work on their own when necessary. Artists must be willing to work long hours to meet deadlines.

EXPLORING

One of the best ways to learn about a career as a supporting artist is to actually try your hand at a variety of animation techniques. If you want to become a storyboard artist, for example, experiment with using storyboarding software or try drawing storyboards for an animated short by hand. The key is to experiment and immerse yourself in the art materials and computer software programs that are used in the field to get hands-on experience. You can also read books and magazines about animation, visit Web sites of animation production companies and studios, and talk to supporting artists about their careers.

EMPLOYERS

Supporting artists are employed by animation, film, and television studios (such as Pixar, DreamWorks Animation SKG, and Walt Disney Animation Studios).

STARTING OUT

Aspiring artists should contact animation companies directly for information on job openings. They can also find job listings at Animation World Network (http://www.awn.com). College career services offices also provide job listings. Participation in an internship will provide aspiring artists with valuable contacts, which could lead to job opportunities.

ADVANCEMENT

Supporting artists can advance in several ways. Talented workers might be assigned more prestigious projects or seek positions at larger companies. Others can continue their education to become art directors, production designers, directors, or animators. Certain workers in this field, such as storyboard artists, have the skills and experience to become animation directors.

EARNINGS

The U.S. Department of Labor does not provide salary information for supporting artists. It does report that multimedia artists and animators earned salaries that ranged from less than $31,570 to $100,390 or more in 2008. Those employed in the motion picture and video industries had mean annual earnings of $71,910.

The Animators Guild Local 839, a union that represents animation professionals in California, conducts an annual survey of its members. It reports that background artists and texture painters earned weekly salaries in 2009 that ranged from $1,490 to $2,774. Inbetweeners had average weekly earnings of $1,100; inkers, $1,099; painters, $1,091; and stylists, $1,313.

Benefits for full-time workers include vacation and sick time, health, and sometimes dental, insurance, and pension or 401(k) plans. Self-employed supporting artists must provide their own benefits.

WORK ENVIRONMENT

Supporting artists usually work in well-lighted design studios. The atmosphere is usually creative, but fast-paced. Artists may work under constant deadline pressure, and may be asked to work nights and weekends to complete projects.

OUTLOOK

Employment for supporting artists should continue to be good during the next decade. They play a key role in the creation of animated films, shorts, music videos, and commercials. One thing that aspiring supporting artists need to keep in mind is that advances in technology will continue to change the way animated films and products are created. This will require them to continue to upgrade their skills throughout their careers. Those with the most up-to-date skills will have the best employment opportunities in this highly competitive industry.

FOR MORE INFORMATION

For information on union membership and earnings, contact
Animators Guild Local 839
1105 North Hollywood Way
Burbank, CA 91505-2528
Tel: 818-845-7500
Email: info@animationguild.org
http://www.animationguild.org

For industry information, contact
International Animated Film Society-ASIFA Hollywood
2114 West Burbank Boulevard
Burbank, CA 91506-1232
Tel: 818-842-8330
Email: info@asifa-hollywood.org
http://www.asifa-hollywood.org

This union represents scenic artists, scenic and production designers, art directors, costume designers, lighting designers, sound designers, projection designers, computer artists, industrial workers, and art department coordinators working in film, television, industrial shows, theatre, opera, ballet, commercials, and exhibitions.
United Scenic Artists Local USA 829
29 West 38th Street, 15th Floor
New York, NY 10018-5504
212-581-0300
http://www.usa829.org

This nonprofit organization represents "visual effects practitioners including artists, technologists, model makers, educators, studio leaders, supervisors, public relations/marketing specialists, and producers in all areas of entertainment from film, television and commercials to music videos and games." Visit its Web site for information about festivals and presentations and news about the industry.
Visual Effects Society
5535 Balboa Boulevard, Suite 205
Encino, CA 91316-1544
Tel: 818-981-7861
Email: info@visualeffectssociety.com
http://www.visualeffectssociety.com

Testers

OVERVIEW

Testers examine new or modified computer and video game applications to evaluate whether or not they perform at the desired level. Testers also verify that different tasks and levels within a game function properly and progress in a consistent manner. Their work entails trying to find glitches in games and sometimes crashing the game completely. Testers keep very close track of the combinations they enter so that they can replicate the situation in order to remedy it. Testers also offer opinions on the user-friendliness of video and computer games. Any problems they find or suggestions they have are reported in detail both verbally and in writing to supervisors.

According to the Entertainment Software Association, approximately 145 million people in the United States play video and computer games.

HISTORY

Over the years technology has continued to shrink computer size and increase speed at an unprecedented rate. The video game industry first emerged in the 1970s. Early engineers included Ralph Baer and Steve Russell. Magnavox first manufactured Russell's TV video game *Odyssey* in 1972.

Atari and Sega were the prominent manufacturers of video games throughout the 1970s and 1980s. Nintendo gained popularity in the mid-1980s, and continues to be a dominant player in the industry. Although gaming is a relatively new industry, companies such as Magnavox and Nintendo are more than a century old.

The field of testing and quality assurance has changed with the advent of automated testing tools. There will always be a need for game testers, however, since they, not a computer, are best suited to judge a game from a user's point of view.

THE JOB

The primary responsibilities of game testers are game testing and report writing. Testers work with all sorts of games, including handheld electronic devices, computer programs, and traditional video games, which are played on the television screen. As technology advances, testers are responsible for games on more compact electronic devices, such as mobile telephones and palm-sized electronic organizers, as well as online games.

Before video game manufacturers can introduce a game to the consumer market, they must run extensive tests on its quality and effectiveness. Failing to do so thoroughly can be very expensive, resulting in poor sales when games are defective or do not perform well. Video and computer games require extremely detailed technical testing.

Games to be tested arrive in the testing department after programmers and software engineers have finished the initial version. Each game is assigned a specific number of tests, and the game testers go to work. To test a game, testers play it over and over again for hours, trying to make moves quickly or slowly to "crash" it. A program crashes if it completely stops functioning due to, among other things, an inability to process incoming commands. Testers spend the majority of their time identifying smaller glitches or discrepancies in games, which are known as "bugs."

Game testers must clearly report any bugs that they find in a game. They keep detailed records of the hours logged working on individual programs. These are called bug reports. Bug reports are based on the tester's observations about how well the game performed in different situations. Testers must always imagine how typical, nontechnical users would judge it. Game testers can also make suggestions about design improvements.

Prior to being employed in this field, it is important for potential game testers to carefully observe how different types of people play games. This will help to ensure that suggestions and evaluations reflect more than just personal bias.

In addition, testers verify that video games perform in accordance with designer specifications and user requirements. This includes checking not only the game's functionality (how it will work), but also its network performance (how it will work with other products), installation (how to put it in), and configuration (how it is set up).

Once game testers make sure that the correct tests are run and the reports written, they send the game back to the programmers for revisions and correction. Some testers have direct contact with the programmers. After evaluating a product, they might meet with programmers to describe the problems they encountered and suggest ways for solving glitches. Others report solely to a game testing coordinator or supervisor.

The goal is to make the video games and computer programs more efficient, user-friendly, fun, and visually exciting. Testers keep track of the precise combinations of controller movements, keystrokes, and mouse clicks that made the program err or crash. These records must be very precise because they enable supervisors and programmers to replicate the problem. Then they can better isolate its source and begin to design a solution.

Game testers work closely with a team of development professionals. *Computer and video game developers* and *designers* create and develop new games. They delegate responsibilities to *artists, writers,* and *audio engineers* who work together to produce the developer's desired vision of each game. These professionals creatively collaborate their ideas of style and flow to make each game a polished and engaging finished project. *Programmers* have to reproduce the bugs before they fix them. *Producers* keep the video game's progress on schedule and within budget.

REQUIREMENTS

High School

Interested in becoming a video game tester? If so, then take as many computer classes as possible to become familiar with how to effectively operate computer software and hardware. Math and science courses are very helpful for learning the necessary analytical skills. English and speech classes will help you improve your verbal and written communication skills, which are also essential to the success of video game testers.

Postsecondary Training

It is debatable whether or not a bachelor's degree is necessary to become a video game tester. Many companies require a bachelor's degree in computer science, while others prefer people who come from the business sector who have a small amount of computer experience because they best match the technical level of the software's typical users. Courses in computer science and psychology are beneficial. Some companies require job seekers to submit a short writing sample when applying for a testing position.

If testers are interested in advancement, however, a bachelor's degree is almost certainly a requirement. Few universities or colleges offer courses on video game testing. As a result, most companies offer in-house training on how to test their particular games. A few specialized schools offer courses such as Introduction to Computer Gaming, Game Testing, and Test Management. A very small number of schools, including DigiPen Institute of Technology (http://www.digipen.edu), exist solely to train digital entertainment developers.

Certification or Licensing

As the gaming and information technology industries become more competitive, it is increasingly important for game testers to demonstrate professionalism in the workplace. Some game development companies encourage testers to earn computer technician certificates. Such certificates can be obtained at community colleges and technical institutes, as well as four-year colleges and universities. Also, QAI Global Institute offers the certified software tester, certified software quality analyst, and certified software business analyst designations to applicants who pass an examination and satisfy other requirements.

Other Requirements

Game testers need strong verbal and written communication skills. They also must show a proficiency in critical and analytical thinking and be able to critique a product diplomatically. Game testers should have an eye for detail, be focused, and have a lot of enthusiasm because sometimes the work is monotonous and repetitive. Testers should definitely enjoy the challenge of breaking the system.

Some companies recommend that testers have some programming skills in languages such as C, C++, SQL, or Visual Basic. The most important thing is that testers understand the gaming business and the testing tools with which they are working. Game testers should also be creative problem solvers.

EXPLORING

Students interested in video game testing and other computer jobs should gain wide exposure to computer systems and video games of all kinds. ST Labs/Data Dimensions Inc. offers the following advice: Become a power user. Get a computer at home, borrow a friend's, or check out the computer lab at your school. First, work on becoming comfortable using Windows programs and learn how to operate all of the computer, including the hardware, thoroughly. Look for bugs in your software at home and practice writing them up.

Secondly, play as many video and computer games as you can. Get good at all different types of games. Learn the differences between games and become familiar with all commands, tasks, and shortcuts.

Keep up with emerging technologies. If you cannot get much hands-on experience, read about the industry. Join a computer group or society. Read books on testing and familiarize yourself with methodology, terminology, the development cycle, and where testing fits in. Subscribe to newsletters or magazines that are related to video game testing, programming, animation, and game design, such as *Game Developer* (http://www.gdmag.com).

If you live in an area where numerous video game development companies are located, like the Silicon Valley in northern California, for example, you might be able to secure a part-time or summer job as a video game tester. An internship with a game development company or any computer-related internship will be a helpful learning experience.

If possible, save up to attend the Game Developers Conference (http://www.gdconf.com) when you are 18 years of age. This is a great chance to network with industry professionals and make yourself known. In addition, investigate the possibility of spending an afternoon with a video game tester to find out what a typical day is like.

EMPLOYERS

Game testers are employed by computer and video game manufacturers. The *Occupational Outlook Quarterly* refers to games as the Wild West of the computer industry, meaning that no two gaming companies are organized in the same way.

Opportunities are best in large cities and suburbs where business and industry are active. Many testers work for video game manufacturers, a cluster of which are located in Silicon Valley in northern California. There is also a concentration of software manufacturers in Boston, Chicago, and Atlanta.

STARTING OUT

Positions in the field of video game testing can be obtained several different ways. Many universities and colleges host computer job fairs on campus throughout the year that include representatives from several hardware and software companies. Internships and summer jobs with such corporations are always beneficial and provide experience that will give you the edge over your competition. General computer job fairs are also held throughout the year in larger cities. Some job openings are advertised in newspapers. There are also many online career sites listed on the World Wide Web that post job openings, salary surveys, and current employment trends.

ADVANCEMENT

Game testers are considered entry-level positions in most companies. After acquiring experience and industry knowledge, testers might advance to any number of professions within the gaming industry. Project managers, game test coordinators, game designers, developers, and programmers are among the possibilities.

EARNINGS

According to *Game Developer* magazine, quality assurance workers in the gaming industry earned median annual salaries of $30,278 in 2008. Salaries ranged from $25,142 to those with three or fewer years' experience to $43,056 for those with six or more years on the job. Salary.com reports that software quality assurance workers earned salaries that ranged from less than $44,919 to $86,257 or more in 2009.

Most testers receive paid vacation and sick leave and are eligible to participate in group insurance and retirement benefit plans.

WORK ENVIRONMENT

Game testers work in game development studios. They play games for a living, and this work can be very fun and entertaining. However, the work is also generally repetitive and even monotonous. If a game is being tested, for example, a tester may have to play it for hours until it finally crashes, if at all. This might seem like great fun, but most testers agree that even the newest, most exciting game loses its appeal after several hours. This aspect of the job proves to be very frustrating and boring for some individuals.

Video game developers may put in long hours in order to meet deadlines. Their work hours usually include nights or weekends. During the final stages before a game goes into mass production and packaging, however, testers are frequently called on to work overtime.

Since video game testing work involves keeping very detailed records, the job can also be stressful. For example, if a tester works on a game for several hours, he or she must be able to recall at any moment the last few moves or keystrokes entered in case the program crashes. This requires long periods of concentration, which can be tiring.

Meeting with supervisors, programmers, and developers to discuss ideas for the games can be intellectually stimulating. At these times, testers should feel at ease communicating with superiors. On the other end, testers who field customer complaints on the telephone may be forced to bear the brunt of customer dissatisfaction, an almost certain source of stress. The video game industry is always changing, so testers should be prepared to work for many companies throughout their careers.

OUTLOOK

The number of positions in the gaming industry is expected to grow faster than the average through 2016. According to the Entertainment Software Association (ESA), computer and video game sales reached $9.5 billion in 2007, and are expected to maintain steady growth.

The push toward premarket perfection will also help to keep the video game testing profession strong. To stay competitive, companies are refining their procedures to ever-higher levels. One thing is for sure—the video game industry is here to stay. According to the ESA, 53 percent of the most frequent computer and video game players expect to be playing games as much or more 10 years from now as they do today.

FOR MORE INFORMATION

For industry information, contact the following associations:
Entertainment Software Association
575 Seventh Street, NW, Suite 300
Washington, DC 20004-1611
Email: esa@theesa.com
http://www.theesa.com

Software & Information Industry Association
1090 Vermont Avenue, NW, 6th Floor
Washington, DC 20005-4095
Tel: 202-289-7442
http://www.siia.net

To check out video game reviews, learn about classic games, and read about school programs in this industry, visit
GameDev.Net
http://www.gamedev.net

For information on careers and education, student memberships, and to read Careers in Computer Science and Computer Engineering, *contact*
IEEE Computer Society
2001 L Street NW, Suite 700
Washington, DC 20036-4910
Tel: 202-371-0101
Email: help@computer.org
http://www.computer.org

For information on careers in the computer and game development industry, contact
International Game Developers Association
19 Mantua Road
Mt. Royal, NJ 08061-1006
Tel: 856-423-2990
http://www.igda.org

For information on certification, contact
QAI Global Institute
2101 Park Center Drive, Suite 200
Orlando, FL 32835-7614
Tel: 407-363-1112
qaiusa@qaiglobal.com
http://www.qaiglobalinstitute.com

Writers

QUICK FACTS

School Subjects
Computer science
English

Personal Skills
Communication/ideas
Technical/scientific

Work Environment
Primarily indoors
One location with some
travel

Minimum Education Level
Bachelor's degree

Salary Range
$28,020 to $55,000 to
$106,630+

Certification or Licensing
None available

Outlook
About as fast as the average

DOT
131

GOE
01.02.01

NOC
5121

O*NET-SOC
27-3022.00, 27-3042.00,
27-3043.04

OVERVIEW

Animation writers who work for magazines, newspapers, book publishers, game and animation Web sites, and related employers write articles, reviews, and books about computer and video games, animated films and television shows, game platforms, companies, industry trends, and other topics. Other animation writers work for game companies and animation studios and write content for user manuals, marketing campaigns, and Web sites. Some writers may be full-time salaried workers, but many are employed on a freelance basis.

Some writers known as *scriptwriters* write scripts for computer and video games, television shows, films, and commercials. For more information on this type of writer, see the Scriptwriters article.

HISTORY

The first animated cartoon was created in 1892 by Émile Reynaud, a French science teacher. Motion pictures (including animation) became increasingly popular in the early 1900s, with the advent of movie houses and emergence of early film studios. As the film industry grew, so did the number of publications that began to cover this fast-growing and glamorous industry. Some, such as *Variety* (founded in 1905) and *Hollywood Reporter* (1930), are still reporting on the film industry today. These and other magazines featured articles about animation techniques and animation pioneers such as Winsor McCay, Max Fleischer, Chuck Jones, and Walt Disney. Developments in technology created an animation renaissance in the late 1980s and early 1990s, and animation magazines such as *Animation Magazine* (1986) and *Animation Journal* (1991) were founded to report on and detail technological and creative developments in the field.

Ever since the dawn of the commercial game industry in the 1970s, writers have been employed by game companies and developers to write technical documentation, advertising copy, and any other text that was required to produce and sell video games and consoles. Although video games became immensely popular by the late 1970s, the first magazine devoted entirely to gaming wasn't founded until 1981. *Electronic Games* had its origins in a columnist named Bill Kunkel—a professional musician and comic book scriptwriter who wrote for *Video* magazine in the late 1970s. *Electronic Games* was the industry leader until it ceased publication in 1985. Despite continued growth in the industry in the 1980s and early 1990s, there were relatively few magazines specifically devoted to computer and video gaming. The emergence of the Internet, improvements in game technology, and steady increases in game sales created strong interest in games, new technology, and the industry as a whole. Publications such as *Game Informer* (1991) and *Game Developer* (1994) were founded to serve the needs of industry professionals, as well as the interests of people who played the games. Today, writers are employed by dozens of print and online magazines that focus on the ever-changing computer and video game industry.

Books to Read for Aspiring Writers

Bateman, Chris, ed. *Game Writing: Narrative Skills for Videogames*. Florence, Ky.: Charles River Media, 2006.

Despain, Wendy, ed. *Professional Techniques for Video Game Writing*. Wellesley, Mass.: A K Peters Ltd., 2008.

Dille, Flint, and John Zuur Platten. *The Ultimate Guide to Video Game Writing and Design*. Los Angeles: Lone Eagle, 2008.

Marx, Christy. *Writing for Animation, Comics, and Games*. St. Louis, Mo.: Focal Press, 2006.

Muir, Shannon. *Gardner's Guide to Writing and Producing Animation*. Washington, D.C.: Garth Gardner Company, 2007.

Sheldon, Lee. *Character Development and Storytelling for Games*. Florence, Ky.: Course Technology PTR, 2004.

Wright, Jean. *Animation Writing and Development: From Script Development to Pitch*. St. Louis, Mo.: Focal Press, 2005.

In addition to the print media, the broadcasting industry has contributed to the development of the professional animation writer. Radio, television, and the Internet are sources of information, education, and entertainment that provide employment for thousands of animation writers.

THE JOB

Animation writers who work for print and online publishing companies cover a wide variety of topics. They write about the major players (famous directors, animators, and producers), companies (such as Nintendo or Walt Disney Animation Studios), industry trends (anime, computer-generated imagery, etc.), popular films and computer and video games, genres, events (Game Developers Conference, animation festivals, etc.), history, and any other topic that relates to these fields. The nature of their work is as varied as the venues for which they write: newspapers, magazines, books, and Web sites and blogs. Some animation writers also appear on television and radio talk shows and in documentaries.

Staff writers are employed by magazines and newspapers to write news stories, feature articles, and columns about the animation industry. First they come up with an idea for an article from their own interests or are assigned a topic by an editor. The topic is of relevance to the particular publication; for example, a writer for an animation magazine may be assigned an article on the Academy Award for animation. A writer for a video game magazine may come up with the idea of interviewing one of the founders of Atari, a pioneer in the video game industry, or propose writing a review of the latest version of *Call of Duty*. A writer for a weekly entertainment section in a newspaper may be assigned to interview the well-known voice actor in Pixar's latest animated hit or write an article about how a popular video game is being turned into an animated feature film.

After writers receive their assignments, they begin gathering as much information as possible about the subject through library research, interviews, the Internet, observation, and other methods. They keep extensive notes from which they will draw material for their project. Once the material has been organized and arranged in logical sequence, writers prepare a written outline. The process of developing a piece of writing is exciting, although it can also involve detailed and solitary work. After researching an idea, a writer might discover that a different perspective or related topic would be more effective, entertaining, or marketable.

When working on an assignment, writers usually submit their outlines to an editor or other company representative for approval.

Then they write a first draft, trying to put the material into words that will have the desired effect on their audience. They often rewrite or polish sections of the material as they proceed, always searching for just the right way of imparting information or expressing an idea or opinion. A manuscript may be reviewed, corrected, and revised numerous times before a final copy is submitted. Even after that, an editor may request additional changes.

Many animation publications are only available online. Writing for this medium is much different than writing for print. Online writers must be able to write in a style that provides information while also engaging the reader's interest. They must pay special attention to the tone and length of an article. Few readers will scroll through screen after screen of text. While online writers do not need to be computer geniuses, they do need to know what computer and Internet tools can make their articles more interesting. Frequently, online writers incorporate highlighted key words, lists, pop-up boxes or windows, and hypertext links in their articles. These items make the articles visually appealing and easy to read.

Animation columnists or *commentators* analyze news and social issues as they relate to animation industries. They write about events from the standpoint of their own experience or opinion.

Animation critics review animated movies or shorts for print publications and television and radio stations. They tell readers and listeners why or why not, in their opinion, they should spend their money to see a movie. Critics may also interview actors, directors, and other professionals for print or online articles and broadcast interviews. Some critics, such as Roger Ebert, became celebrities in their own right. *Game industry critics* review computer and video games to help readers decide which ones to play, buy, or avoid. They also review gaming hardware, consoles, and related equipment.

Some writers are employed by game companies, game developers, and animation studios. *Technical writers* employed in the game industry prepare a wide variety of documents and materials. They might write content for user guides; instructional online game videos; training manuals; package copy and game summaries; installation instructions for software, hardware, or related materials; and Help and Technical Support sections on company Web sites. Others may write consumer publications published by game companies such as Nintendo. *Copywriters* write advertising copy for computer and video games or movie packaging, company Web sites, and print, radio, Internet, and television advertisements.

Scriptwriters write computer and video games, animated films and shorts, animated television shows, and commercials that feature animation. See the article Scriptwriters for more information on this career.

Writers can be employed either as in-house staff or as freelancers. Pay varies according to experience and the position, but freelancers must provide their own office space and equipment such as computers and fax machines. Freelancers also are responsible for keeping tax records, sending out invoices, negotiating contracts, and providing their own health insurance.

REQUIREMENTS

High School

While in high school, build a broad educational foundation by taking courses in English, literature, foreign languages, history, general science, social studies, computer science, and typing. The ability to type is almost a requisite for many positions in the journalism field, as is familiarity with computers. If you are interested in becoming an animation writer, you should watch as many animated films or play as many video games as possible, as well as read publications on animation and gaming.

Postsecondary Training

Competition for journalistic writing jobs almost always demands the background of a college education. Many employers prefer you have a broad liberal arts background or majors in English, literature, history, philosophy, or one of the social sciences. Other employers desire communications or journalism training in college. Occasionally a master's degree in a specialized writing field may be required. A number of schools offer courses in journalism, and some of them offer courses or majors in newspaper and magazine writing, publication management, book publishing, and writing for the Internet. If you are interested in animation writing, you might want to consider a major, or at least a minor, in a film-, computer game-, or animation-related area. Game manual writers and technical writers might be required to have an advanced degree in computer science, engineering, or a related discipline.

Other Requirements

To be a successful animation writer, you should be creative and able to express ideas clearly, have broad general knowledge, be skilled in research techniques, have a love of animated films or computer and video games, and be computer literate. Other assets include curiosity, persistence, initiative, resourcefulness, and an accurate memory. For some jobs—on a newspaper, for example, where the activity is hectic and deadlines are short—the ability to concentrate and produce under pressure is essential. Animation critics and columnists need to be confident about their opinions and able to accept criticism from others who may not agree with their views.

EXPLORING

If you are interested in becoming a game writer, you should play as many computer and video games as possible. Become familiar with the various gaming companies, platforms, and trends in the business. Pick your favorite (or least favorite) game and write a review of its best and worst features. Consider the game's audio, art design, animation, playability, and other factors when writing your review.

Reading industry publications is an excellent way to learn about animation-related industries. Suggested publications include *Variety* (http://www.variety.com), *Hollywood Reporter* (http://www.hollywoodreporter.com), *Premiere* (http://www.premiere.com), *Entertainment Weekly* (http://www.ew.com/ew), *Animation Journal* (http://www.animationjournal.com), and *Animation World* (http://www.awn.com/magazines/animation-world-magazine). If you are particularly interested in working in the game industry, read the following publications: *Game Developer* (http://www.gdmag.com), *GameZone Online* (http://www.gamezone.com), *Computer Graphics World* (http://www.cgw.com), *GameInformer* (http://www.gameinformer.com), and *VideoGameNews* (http://videogamenews.com). You also might want to read the online resource "Breaking In: Preparing For Your Career in Games," which is available at the International Game Developers Association's Web site (http://archives.igda.org/breakingin). It offers an overview of game industry careers (including writer), profiles of workers in the field, and other resources.

As a high school or college student, you can test your interest and aptitude in the field of writing by working as a reporter or writer on school newspapers, yearbooks, and literary magazines. Perhaps you could write movie reviews for your school newspaper or an article about a particular video game for a school magazine. There are also many Web sites where amateur film critics or game reviewers can post their reviews. Many online game publications solicit reviews and short articles from young people. Most of these do not pay or only offer a small payment or game tokens, but they are excellent ways to hone your writing and have your opinions read by a larger audience. Reputable sites often will provide clips of published work, which you can use to help you develop your portfolio. Of course, you can always write reviews and articles on your own for practice.

Small community newspapers often welcome contributions from outside sources, although they may not have the resources to pay for them.

Be sure to take as many writing courses and workshops as you can to help sharpen your writing skills. You might also consider picking up a copy of *A Short Guide to Writing About Film* for some useful tips.

Information on writing as a career may also be obtained by visiting the offices of local newspapers and game publishers and interviewing some of the people who work there. Career conferences and other guidance programs frequently include speakers on the entire field of communications from local or national organizations.

EMPLOYERS

Writers work for publishing companies of various sizes. Others work for animation studios or independent game development studios and manufacturers of the various computer and video game platforms. Major entertainment software publishers include Activision Blizzard, Electronic Arts, Nintendo of America, Atari, Sony, THQ, Take-Two Interactive, Microsoft, and Konami Digital Entertainment-America. In addition to these large companies, there are many small to mid-level software publishers. Large animation companies include Blue Sky Studios, Rhythm & Hues Studios, Walt Disney Animation Studios, Pixar, Lucasfilm Animation, Warner Bros. Animation Studios, Sony Pictures Animation, and DreamWorks Animation SKG. Visit Animation Industry Database (http://aidb.com) for a database of thousands of animation-related companies.

STARTING OUT

You will need a good amount of experience to gain a high-level position in the field. Nearly all writers start out in entry-level positions. These jobs may be listed with college career services offices, or they may be obtained by applying directly to the employment departments of the individual publishers or game or broadcasting companies. Graduates who previously served internships with these companies often have the advantage of knowing someone who can give them a personal recommendation. Want ads in newspapers and trade journals are another source for jobs. Because of the competition for positions, however, few vacancies are listed with public or private employment agencies.

Employers in the field of journalism usually are interested in samples of published writing. These are often assembled in an organized portfolio or scrapbook. Bylined, or signed, articles are more credible (and, as a result, more useful) than stories whose source is not identified.

Beginning positions as a junior writer usually involve library research, preparation of rough drafts for part or all of a report, cataloging, and other related writing tasks. These are generally carried on under the supervision of a senior writer.

You can apply for employment directly to game companies or publishing companies that produce gaming publications. Be sure to research these companies first to learn more about their products or editorial focus. Don't send your resume and writing samples to every employer that has a job listing. Look for work settings that match your interests and abilities.

There are many Web sites that have job listings for game writers. These include GameJobs (http://www.gamejobs.com), Animation World Network (http://jobs.awn.com), and Gamasutra (http://www.gamasutra.com). Many people also attend the annual Game Developers Conference (http://www.gdconf.com) to network and learn more about internship and job opportunities.

ADVANCEMENT

Most writers find their first jobs as editorial, production, or research assistants. Advancement may be more rapid in small media companies, where beginners learn by doing a little bit of everything and may be given writing tasks immediately. At large publishers or broadcast companies, duties are usually more compartmentalized. Assistants in entry-level positions are assigned such tasks as research and fact checking, but it generally takes much longer to advance to full-scale writing duties.

Promotion into higher-level positions may come with the assignment of more important articles and stories to write, or it may be the result of moving to another company. Mobility among employees in this field is common. A staff writer at a small magazine publisher may switch to a similar position at a more prestigious publication.

As technical writers gain experience, they move into more challenging and responsible positions. At first, they may work on simple documents or are assigned to work on sections of a document. As they demonstrate their proficiency and skills, they are given more complex assignments and are responsible for more activities. Technical writers who show good project management skills, leadership abilities, and good interpersonal skills may become supervisors or managers. Technical writers can also move into the position of senior writer, which involves increased responsibilities and may include supervision of other workers.

Freelance or self-employed writers earn advancement in the form of larger fees as they gain exposure and establish their reputations.

EARNINGS

Writers in the game industry with less than three years' experience earned average salaries of $51,731 in 2008, according to *Game Developer* magazine. Those with three to six years' experience averaged $59,167.

The U.S. Department of Labor reports that writers in all fields earned salaries that ranged from less than $28,020 to more than $106,630 in 2008. It reports the following mean annual salaries for writers by industry: motion picture and video, $98,820; advertising, $71,640; television broadcasting, $63,330; and newspaper, periodical, book, and directory publishers, $51,980.

In 2008 technical writers earned salaries that ranged from less than $36,500 to $97,460 or more. Median annual earnings for technical writers were $61,620. Those employed by software publishers had mean annual earnings of $71,590.

In addition to their salaries, many writers earn income from freelance work. Freelance earnings vary widely. Full-time, established freelance writers may earn more than $75,000 a year. Part-time writers may be paid on a per-review or per-article basis. These one-time fees may range from as little as $5 to $50 for a game review to $50 to $300 or more for a full-length article.

Typical benefits may be available for full-time, salaried employees, including sick leave, vacation pay, and health, life, and disability insurance. Retirement plans may also be available, and some companies may match employees' contributions. Some companies may also offer stock-option plans.

Freelance writers do not receive benefits and are responsible for their own medical, disability, and life insurance. They do not receive vacation pay, and when they aren't working, they aren't generating income. Retirement plans must also be self-funded and self-directed.

WORK ENVIRONMENT

Working conditions vary for writers. Although their workweek usually runs 35 to 40 hours, many writers work overtime. A publication that is issued frequently has more deadlines closer together, creating greater pressures to meet them. The work is especially hectic on newspapers, which operate seven days a week. Writers often work nights and weekends to meet deadlines or to cover a late-developing story.

Most writers work independently, but they often must cooperate with editors, artists, photographers, and rewriters who may have widely differing ideas of how the materials should be prepared and presented. Physical surroundings range from comfortable private offices to noisy, crowded newsrooms filled with other workers typing and talking on the telephone. Some writers must confine their research to the library or telephone interviews, but others may travel to other cities or countries or to local sites, such as game companies, animation studios, animation festivals, game conferences, or other business settings.

OUTLOOK

Writers will continue to be needed in the computer and video game industry to write advertising copy, game manuals, articles, or books about games and trends in the field. Opportunities will be especially strong for writers with online publishing experience. Employment will also be good for technical writers because the number of computer and video games produced each year continues to increase. The U.S. Department of Labor predicts that employment for writers employed in all industries will grow about as fast as the average for all occupations through 2016.

Employment of writers and authors in the motion picture and video industries is expected to increase faster than the average for all careers through 2016, according to the U.S. Department of Labor. There is a steady demand for writers that create advertising copy, write articles and books about the animation industry, and create content for industry and other Web sites. Competition for jobs will be very strong since many people want to enter this field. Employment for writers in the advertising industry is expected to grow about as fast as the average through 2016.

FOR MORE INFORMATION

The following organizations represent film critics in cities across the United States:

Chicago Film Critics Association
PO Box 280
Arlington Heights, IL 60006-0280

Tel: 847-427-4530
Email: critics@chicagofilmcritics.org
http://www.chicagofilmcritics.org

The Los Angeles Film Critics Association
http://www.lafca.net

New York Film Critics Circle
http://www.nyfcc.com

For industry information, contact the following associations:
Entertainment Software Association
575 Seventh Street, NW, Suite 300
Washington, DC 20004-1611
Email: esa@theesa.com
http://www.theesa.com

Software & Information Industry Association
1090 Vermont Avenue, NW, 6th Floor
Washington, DC 20005-4095
Tel: 202-289-7442
http://www.siia.net

Visit the following Web site for comprehensive information on jour-
nalism careers, summer programs, and college journalism programs:
High School Journalism
http://www.highschooljournalism.org

For information on careers in the computer and game development
industry, contact
International Game Developers Association
19 Mantua Road
Mt. Royal, NJ 08061-1006
Tel: 856-423-2990
http://www.igda.org

The OFCS is an international association of Internet-based film
critics and journalists.
The Online Film Critics Society (OFCS)
Email: admissions@ofcs.org
http://ofcs.rottentomatoes.com

For additional information regarding online writing and journalism, check out the following Web site:
Online News Association
Email: info@journalists.org
http://journalists.org?

For information on awards and internships, contact
Society of Professional Journalists
Eugene S. Pulliam National Journalism Center
3909 North Meridian Street
Indianapolis, IN 46208-4011
Tel: 317-927-8000
http://www.spj.org

Index

Entries and page numbers in **bold** indicate major treatment of a topic.